Official Cambridge Exam Preparation

Kid's Box

New Generation

British English

Caroline Nixon &
Michael Tomlinson

CAMBRIDGE

Pupil's Book

with eBook

5

Language summary

	Key vocabulary	Key language	Sounds and life skills

Welcome to our blog
page 4

School subjects: *art, computer studies, English, French, geography, German, history, maths, science, Spanish, sport, music*

School: *competition, dictionary, exam, language, lesson, prize, study, subject*

Like/Love + -ing/nouns, 'd like + infinitive

Present simple questions and short answers: *Do you live near your school? Yes, I do. / No, I don't.*

Connected speech

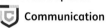 Communication

---

1 Time for television
page 10

The time: *half, o'clock, past, quarter, to*

TV programmes: *action film, cartoon, comedy, documentary, news, quiz show, rock music video, sport, weather*

TV: *channel, episode, series, stream, turn on*

Adjectives: *amazing, bad, boring, exciting, funny, good, interesting*

The time: *What time is it? It's quarter past one.*

Consonant clusters
sh and *ch*
(*finish, channel*)

 Collaboration

Media: nature documentaries   page 16

---

2 People at work
page 18

Jobs: *actor, artist, cook, dentist, doctor, football player, journalist, mechanic, nurse, pilot, sports commentator, video game designer, writer*

Plans, intentions and predictions with *going to*: *What's William going to be when he grows up? He's going to be a designer.*

The /ə/ sound
(*doctor*)

 Creative thinking

Social science: safety procedures   page 24

Review units 1 and 2   page 26

---

3 City life
page 28

City life: *airport, bridge, castle, fire station, gym, hotel, museum, playground, police station, post office, prison, restaurant, road, stadium, street, taxi, theatre, zoo*

Directions: *across, along, corner, left, past, right, straight on*

Directions: *Go along/across/ straight on/past, Take the first/ second/third street, Turn left/ right into/at/on the corner*

Prepositions: *behind, between, next to, opposite*

Consonant clusters
str, st and *sp*
(*street, stadium, sports*)

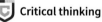 Critical thinking

Geography: city life   page 34

---

4 Disaster!
page 36

Disasters: *earthquake, hurricane, iceberg, lightning, storm, tsunami, volcano*

Verbs: *break (leg), catch fire, cut, destroy, drop, erupt, fall down, hit, hurt, lose*

Months

Past continuous and past simple: *I was having a picnic when it started to rain. What were you doing?*

The vowel sounds
(*sailing, sea, sky, hello, rescue*)

 Creative thinking

Geography and History: natural landscapes   page 42

Review units 3 and 4   page 44

	Key vocabulary	Key language	Sounds and life skills
5 Material things page 46	**Materials:** *brick, card, fur, glass, gold, grass, leather, man-made, metal, natural, paper, plastic, recycle, rubber, silver, stone, sugar, wood, wool*	**Describing objects:** *What's the school made of? I think it's made of stone.*	Connected speech 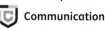 Communication

Art: sculptures   page 52

	Key vocabulary	Key language	Sounds and life skills
6 Senses page 54	**Senses:** *hear, see, smell, taste, touch* **Cooking:** *bowl, cheese, cut, flour, fork, ingredients, knife, mix, olives, onion, oven, pepper, pizza, plate, recipe, salami sausage, salt, spoon, topping*	**Describing sensations:** *What does it look like? It looks like a cat's nose.*	Sentence stress Creative thinking

Science: sound waves   page 60

Review units 5 and 6   page 62

	Key vocabulary	Key language	Sounds and life skills
7 Natural world page 64	**Nature:** *beetle, bin, butterfly, clean-up, endangered species, extinct, field, ground, habitat, in danger, insect, protect, rubbish, tree* **Describing species:** *female, male, spots, spotted, striped, stripes, wing*	**Giving advice:** *How should we look after our world? People shouldn't drop their rubbish. They should put it in a bin. I think we should all recycle bottles. Yes, I agree. / No, I don't agree.*	Sentence stress 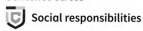 Social responsibilities

Geography: endangered species and conservation   page 70

	Key vocabulary	Key language	Sounds and life skills
8 World of sport page 72	**Sports:** *athletics, badminton, cycling, golf, ice skating, racing, running, sailing, skiing, sledging, snowboarding, volleyball* **Seasons:** *spring, summer, autumn, winter*	**Present perfect for life experiences:** *Have you ever won a prize? Yes, I have. / No, I haven't. I've never won a prize.* **Present perfect for recently completed actions:** *He's visited his grandmother this afternoon.* **Present perfect for completed actions with present relevance:** *He hasn't done his homework.*	Endings /t/, /d / and /id/ (*jumped, climbed, decided*) Emotional development

Physical education: aerobic and anaerobic exercise   page 78

Review units 7 and 8   page 80

Welcome to our blog

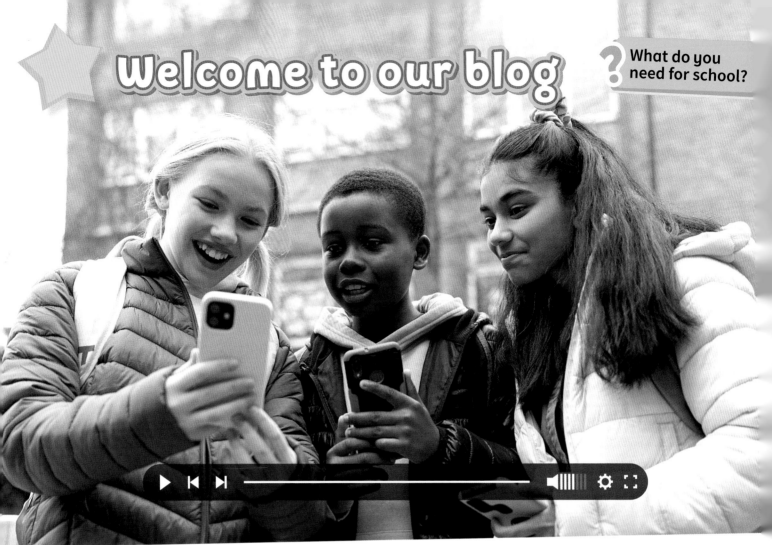

 Who gets an exciting message? Watch and check.

 Watch again. Order.

1 Can we write about sport and technology?
2 Let's meet outside school at four o'clock.
3 Well, it's our first day back at school, so let's write about that.
4 Did you have a good holiday? [1]
5 It's about a new school blog.
6 Are you ready for a new school year?

STUDY

How are things?
Are you ready for a new school year?
Can we write about sport?

 Answer the questions.

1 What are the children's names?
2 Why wasn't Meera online?
3 Where are they?

4 What's the competition for?
5 What's the prize for?
6 What can they write about?

 Ask and answer.

1 What did you think of Meera's idea for a blog post about their first day at school?
2 Imagine you are writing a blog post for a competition. What would you like to write about?

Language: present simple questions and short answers

1 ▶ **Can you remember the last lesson? Watch the language video.**

 2 **Read and answer.**

All about us

Kid's Box is an exciting new blog for young people. Meera, Stella and Lenny want to write a post for the blog. They all go to the same school. It's called 'City School'.

Meera
I'm ten. I live near the school, so I walk in every day. I have lunch at school with my friends. I love drawing and taking photos, so I want to put my photos in the blog and write about the natural world.

Stella
I'm ten. I live in a village outside the town, so I catch a bus to school every morning. I like singing and music and I enjoy playing the piano. I love reading and studying. I'd like to write about music and science in the blog.

Lenny
I'm eleven years old. I always ride my bike to school. I sometimes have breakfast in the school breakfast club before my classes. I love playing football and basketball. I'm also interested in computers. I'd like to write about sport and technology in the blog.

1 What's **Kid's Box**?
2 Which school do they go to?
3 What does Meera love doing?
4 How old is Stella?
5 What would Stella like to write about?
6 How does Lenny go to school?
7 Who's interested in technology?
8 Who's the oldest, Meera, Stella or Lenny?

 3 🎧 2 **Listen and say the name.** 🎧 1 Who lives near the school? Meera does.

 4 **Ask and answer.** Do you live near your school? No, I don't.

live / near school
lunch / home
play / musical instrument
like / sport
read / magazines
use / internet

 5 📝 **Write more questions.**

1 **Read the blog. What's their favourite subject?**

ALL BLOGS   MY BLOG   NEW POST

Kid's Box
Reports

For our first blog post, we went round our school to find out more about what we learn.

We all study these school subjects: maths, English, science, music, sport, art and computer studies.

Our school

Older students have to study more school **subjects** and take important **exams**.

Science is an important subject, so we study it every day. This year we're learning about plants and the human body.

We study a **second language**. We can choose French, German or Spanish.

In our **geography lessons**, we learn about different people and their countries.

We use the **dictionaries** in the school library to help us to understand new words.

The best subject is **history**. We love learning about the past!

We all agree that the best thing about school at the moment is the blog **competition**. We all want to win that **prize**!

 2 **Read again and say 'same' or 'different' for your class.**

1 At City School, they all study music.
2 Older students take important exams.
3 They can choose a second language.
4 There are dictionaries in the school library.

5 They study science every day.
6 They are learning about plants and the human body.
7 They learn about different people and their countries.
8 They think history is better than geography.

 3 **Ask and answer.**

1 Which languages can you learn at school?

I can learn French at my school.

2 What's your favourite school subject?

My favourite school subject is English.

1 🎧 3 **Listen and say the subject.**

🎧 **1** A lot of people think the capital of Australia is Sydney, but it isn't. It's Canberra.

Geography.

 **2** **Read and choose the right words.**

1 We study the past in **science / geography / history**.
2 French, Spanish and German are **languages / exams / maths**.
3 When we don't understand a word, we can use **a book / a dictionary / art**.

4 We study plants and the human body in **maths / sport / science**.
5 We learn about people and countries in **geography / computer studies / music**.
6 Teachers sometimes find out what we know by giving us **subjects / computers / exams**.

3 🎧 ▶ 4–5 **Read and write. Listen and check. Then do karaoke.**

Because school is cool, it's where we go
From Monday to Friday, I'm sure you know.
We study and we play, that's what we do.
We do it in the morning and the afternoon!

I really love (1) _____ ,

And I enjoy (2) _____ .

I like to study (3) _____ too!

My favourite subject in the afternoon.

Before lunch we have (4) _____ ,

And then (5) _____ ,

And on Wednesday we do (6) _____ .

That's a class which is too short!

And I like to do (7) _____ ,

Spanish, French and Japanese.

Lots of words in the (8) _____ ,

For me to study and to read.

4 **Read about the school words. What are they?**

With this subject we can learn to talk to people from another country.
In this lesson we learn about plants and the human body.
When we study this we learn about different countries and people.
We use this to learn new words.

 5 📝 **Write three more definitions. Ask and answer.**

With this subject we can learn about numbers and shapes. What is it?

Is it maths?

Yes, it is.

Sounds and life skills
Chatting with friends

 1 ▶ **Watch the video. Where are the young people and how do they feel?**

Pronunciation focus

 2 🎧 6 **Listen and complete.**

STELLA: Hi, Meera. _____ have a good holiday?

MEERA: Yeah, great, thanks.

STELLA: I didn't see you online – _____ ?

MEERA: It's because we didn't have any wi-fi, but I can show you the pictures if you want. Oh, look! Here's Lenny!

STELLA: Hi, Lenny. _____ things?

LENNY: Good thanks, Stella. _____ ready for the new school year?

STELLA: Yeah, _____ .

3 🎧 7 **Listen and circle the words that sound connected. Practise with a partner.**

1 (How are) things?
2 Are you happy to be back?
3 Did you have a good summer?

 4 **In pairs, look at the quiz and add more school holiday activities.**

Find out who ...	Extra information	
_____ travelled by train.	Where? _____	Who with? _____
_____ went to a fair.	Where? _____	What rides? _____
_____ watched a film.	What film? _____	Who with? _____
_____ walked in the countryside.	Where? _____	Who with? _____
_____ played lots of sports.	What sports? _____	Who with? _____

 **Did you have a good holiday?**

 5 **Find a classmate who did each activity. Ask extra questions.**

Useful language

How are things?
Where did you go?
Who did you go with?

Diggory Bones

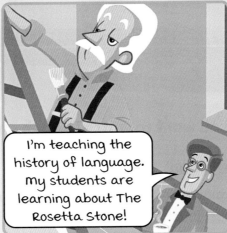

1 **What's Diggory Bones teaching? What's The Baloney Stone?**

1 Time for television

1 ▶ **What TV show do they all want to watch? Watch and check.**

2 ▶ **Watch again. Say 'yes' or 'no'.**

1 The children are in the supermarket at the beginning of the story.
2 The football is on TV at ten past four.
3 The girls want to watch a programme called **Top Talent**.
4 Mr Sharma wants to watch the same programme as them.
5 The golf finishes at twenty to seven.
6 Lenny and Stella have to be home at quarter past six.

> No.

STUDY

It's **quarter to** four.
It's **quarter past** four.

3 **Read and match.**

1 The children are in the kitchen   a   at ten past four.
2 The football is on   b   at twenty to seven.
3 **Top Talent** is on   c   at twenty past four.
4 The children arrive in the living room   d   at twenty-five past four.
5 The golf finishes   e   at quarter past four.
6 Lenny and Stella have to be home   f   at half past six.

4 **Ask and answer.**

1 Would you like to watch **Top Talent**? Why? Why not?
2 What do you and your family do when you want to watch different TV programmes?

1 ▶ **Can you remember the last lesson? Watch the language video.**

 1

 2 **Read and label the clock.**   [ten past   five past   twenty-five to   quarter to]

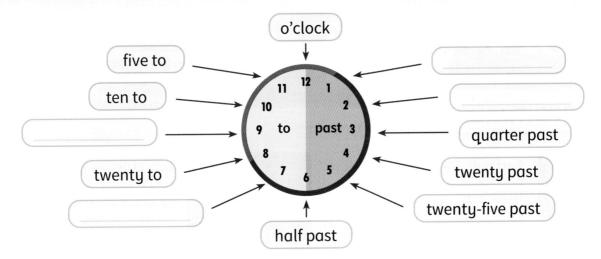

o'clock

five to

ten to

twenty to

half past

quarter past

twenty past

twenty-five past

 3 **What do you do every day? Order.**

wake up

get up

get dressed

go to school

clean my teeth [1]

go to bed

do my homework

have breakfast

 9 **4** **Look at the clocks. Listen and say the letter.**

 1 I have lunch at quarter to one every day.

 a

1
 a    b    c

3
 a    b    c

2
 a    b    c

4
 a    b    c

 5 **Play the game. Ask and answer.**

I get up at this time on Mondays. What time is it?

No.

Yes.

Twenty past seven.

Twenty to eight.

 6 **Write about your day. Write 20–30 words.**

1 **Read the blog. Which programme is on TV at the same time every day?**

ALL BLOGS | MY BLOG | NEW POST

Kid's Box Reports

Today's blog post is about different kinds of TV programmes. You can watch them on TV or **stream** them to your phone or tablet.

TV programmes

Cartoons are moving pictures. Children and grown-ups love them. They can be short programmes or complete films. They're usually funny.

Lots of people enjoy watching **sport** on TV. Some of the most popular sports in the world are football, basketball, tennis and golf. What sports are popular in your country?

We watch the **weather** to find out if it's sunny, rainy, windy or cloudy. What's the weather like today?

A **quiz** is a kind of competition. One person asks others lots of different questions. The winner is the person with the most points.

A **documentary** is a programme which gives us information about our world. It can be about animals, history or geography.

The **news** is about things which are happening in the world. It's on TV at the same time every day.

A **comedy** is a funny programme which makes us laugh. What's your favourite comedy?

We watch a **series** in parts. These parts are called **episodes**. You can sometimes watch an episode every day.

2 **Read again and answer.**

1 Which programme can tell us things about animals?
2 Which programme can be short or a complete film?
3 Which programme is about things which are happening in the world?
4 Which is one of the most popular sports in the world?
5 Which programme can tell us to take an umbrella with us?
6 Which programme is in episodes?
7 Which programme is a kind of competition?
8 Which programmes are funny?

3 **Ask and answer.**

1 What's your favourite TV programme?

> My favourite TV programme is the news.

2 Why do you like it?

> I like learning about what's happening in the world.

3 What's it about?

> It's about the news around the world.

1 10 **Listen and say the programme.**

 1 Goal.   Sport.

> cartoon   comedy   documentary   news
> quiz show   rock music video   ~~sport~~   weather

2 **Choose words to talk about the different programmes.**

> amazing   bad   boring   exciting   funny   good   interesting

> I think quiz shows are more interesting than the weather.

> I think rock music videos are the best.

3 11–12 **Listen and complete the clocks. Listen and check. Then do karaoke.**

I don't like TV, I don't like it much,
But there are some programmes that
I sometimes watch.
On channel one at ⏰ ,

There's a really good documentary
About animals and where they live,
What they do and what they eat.
And on channel four at ⏰ ,

They put on a great cartoon.
At one o'clock and then at ⏰

They show the news and then the weather.
They're not my thing, they're not for me,
But I like the sport at ⏰ .

But what I like, what I love the best,
Are the action films, more than the rest.
They're on at ⏰ ,

And at but I want more.

4 **Read and complete.**

> arrived   ~~four~~   news   past
> turned on   waited

Tim and Jen went to the park last Saturday. They ran on the grass, played with a ball and went on the swings. At ten to ⁽¹⁾ _four_ they sat down because they were tired. They saw a newspaper on the bench. They opened it at the TV page and looked to see what was on the different channels. Tim wanted to go home and watch **Friendly** at half ⁽²⁾_____ four. They went to the bus stop and ⁽³⁾_____. The bus didn't come until quarter past four. They ⁽⁴⁾_____ home at twenty-five to five, ran into the living room and ⁽⁵⁾_____ the TV. The programme wasn't **Friendly**, it was the ⁽⁶⁾_____. They looked at the newspaper again. It was an old one! They showed **Friendly** on Friday, not on Saturday.

Sounds and life skills
Deciding together

1 ► **Watch the video. What is the problem and what do they do about it?**

Pronunciation focus

2 🎧 **13** **Listen and underline the sounds *sh* and *ch*.**

MEERA:	Hi, Dad. Can we please change the channel? We want to watch **Top Talent**.
MR SHARMA:	Oh, I'm sorry, Meera. Not now. The golf's on – and you know I love golf!
STELLA:	What time does it finish, Mr Sharma?
MR SHARMA:	Oh, don't worry. It finishes at twenty to seven!

3 **Think and complete. Practise with a partner.**

A: Can we please change the channel and watch _____ ?

B: No, I'm sorry. I'm watching _____ .

A: What time does it finish?

B: It finishes at _____ .

4 **Look at the TV guide. Which two programmes would you like to watch and why?**

5 In a group, discuss the TV programmes and decide what to watch together.

Channel 1
17.00 Sing Up!
In this evening's semi-final contest, four singers sing their best songs with famous musicians. Vote to see your favourite in next week's finale!

18.30 Film: Starshine
Dr Dark has a plan to take away starlight from the universe. Can five young scientists and one spaceship stop him?

TV DOC 3
18.00 Shark Show
In this documentary, Shark Dave shows us one of the fastest fish on the planet: the shortfin mako.

18.30 Insect Investigation: Explore the world of Magical Dragonflies

19.00 The Curious Chef
Shona travels to China to discover new lunch dishes to cook at home.

SPORT4U Live
17.10 Football Crazy
Live: Sporting Galaxy v Chester City.

18.30 American Basketball Special
Live: New York v Orlando.

Useful language
Can/Can't we watch …?
What time is it on?

1 **What can the thief do with The Baloney Stone program?**
What does Brutus Grabbe want?

1 🎧 15 **Listen and read. Which programme doesn't show real animals?**

FILMING NATURE

There are some great nature documentaries coming out this month, so we wanted to hear from some of the people behind the magic. They told us about how new technology brings viewers closer to nature.

I started working as an underwater camera operator 30 years ago. Making documentaries was very different then. My video camera was big and heavy, with batteries that didn't last long. Unfortunately, there isn't much light underwater, so the cameras didn't film very well. Now, the technology is amazing! We use small, low-light cameras and long-life batteries, so we can stay underwater for longer.

For **Discover the Deep**, I went deeper into the ocean than ever before. I filmed some incredible underwater animals we never knew about!

Adrian Hems, Camera Operator

New technology means we can now make really exciting nature documentaries. In **Migrations**, we used drone cameras to film animals from the air. We film hundreds of animals moving across the land together. In the past, we filmed from a helicopter. Some people still do that, but I think using drones is much better. You can get closer to the animals. In the first episode, I filmed the amazing elephant migration in Botswana.

Lucy Hall, Director of Photography

Working on **How Dinosaurs Lived** was so much fun! I create computer animations of animals and make them look real. Dinosaurs are extinct, so we filmed the landscape they once lived in. I created the dinosaurs with computer-generated images (CGI), and we added them to the landscape. The effects are excellent – much better than the ones I used on films in the past. I created some amazing dinosaur fights!

Ben Sharp, Special Effects Technician

2 **Read again and complete the diagram.**

Past — big, heavy cameras

Present — small, low-light cameras

3 **Which programme sounds more interesting to make and why?**

I'd like to watch **Discover the Deep**. Filming deep underwater sounds amazing!

Creating dinosaurs with special effects must be a lot of fun, so I really want to watch **How Dinosaurs Lived!**

— FIND **OUT MORE** —
What is the most expensive nature documentary ever made?

1 **Read the chat message. Why did they think the programme was interesting?**

DID YOU KNOW...?

The giant squid is one of the world's most difficult animals to film because it lives so deep in the ocean. Camera operators first filmed this sea animal in 2012!

1

12:00   % ▯

← 👤 **Fahad is online**   🔍 🏠 ☰

Quinn

Hi Fahad, how are you?

Yesterday, I watched an amazing documentary called **City Animals**. It's about animals that live in big cities. You can watch it on the **Wildlife Channel** every Sunday.

Last night's episode was about foxes in cities. I found it really interesting because there's a fox that comes into our garden. Look at the photo that I took of it. Isn't it cute?

Some people are frightened of foxes, but they're shy animals. In the documentary, they explained that foxes now live among humans in towns because we are destroying their natural habitat.

You must watch it because you can learn about some really awesome animals. Next week's episode is about owls. The photography is incredible, too!

2 **Underline the adjectives in the chat message in Activity 1.**

3 📝 **In pairs, discuss a nature documentary you know. Write your ideas in your notebook.**

What's the name of the documentary?

What's it about? Why is it interesting?

Learning to write:

Adjectives

We use adjectives to describe things.

My video camera was **big** and **heavy**.

I created some **amazing** dinosaur fights!

Ready to write:

Go to Activity Book page 16.

Project

Make a presentation about a nature documentary.

Media: nature documentaries | 🛡 learning to learn   17

2 People at work

BECOME A DENTIST

BECOME A NURSE
Join our team, ask for more

 1 Why does everyone have to leave the school? Watch and check.

 2 Watch again. Complete the sentences.

1 They're looking around a _____ exhibition.
2 Lenny thinks he's going to be a _____ .
3 Stella thinks she's going to be a _____ .
4 Stella hopes the _____ isn't going to burn down.
5 Meera's going to be a _____ .
6 They're going to write about _____ .

STUDY

I'm **going to be** a vet.
Meera **isn't going to be** a hairdresser.
What **are** we **going to write** about?

 3 Read and order the words.

1 write about / What / for our blog post? / are / we / going to
2 going to / a nurse / be / when I'm older. / I'm
3 a doctor. / going to / Meera / be / isn't
4 The school / isn't / burn down. / going to
5 win / prize! / We're / that / going to
6 do / you / What / tomorrow? / are / going to

 4 Ask and answer.

1 What are Stella, Lenny and Meera going to be? Do you think they will be good at those jobs?
2 What do you think you and your friends are going to be? Why?

18 **Language:** plans, intentions and predictions with *going to*

1 ▶ Can you remember the last lesson? Watch the language video.

2 🎧 ▶ 16–17 Listen and order. Listen again and check. Then do karaoke.

a She's going to help them all,
And work in schools ... ☐

b They're going to do their best,
Then sleep and play. ☐

c They're going to do the job,
Then work all day,
Then sleep and play ... ☐

d She's going to show the kids,
She's going to teach good rules. ☐

f He's going to do his best,
Then sleep and play ... ☐

e They're going to do the job,
They're going to work all day. ☐

g He's going to do the job,
He's going to work all day. ☐ 1

3 Look and say. What are they going to do?

4 Correct the sentences.

a She's going to wash her face.
b They're going to go to a music festival.
c They're going to turn on a computer.
d She's going to play tennis.
e They're going to watch TV.
f He's going to wake up.

> **a** No, she isn't going to wash her face. She's going to brush her teeth.

5 📝 Write two more questions. Then ask your partner.

1 Where are you going to go after school?
2 Who are you going to see this evening?
3 When are you going to do your homework?
4 What time are you going to go to bed tonight?

6 📝 What are you going to do after school? Write 20–30 words.

1 **Read the blog. Which three jobs did George Orwell have?**

ALL BLOGS   MY BLOG   NEW POST

Kid's Box Reports

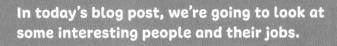
In today's blog post, we're going to look at some interesting people and their jobs.

Interesting jobs

Formula 1 is a car racing competition. It's a team sport. One of the most important people in the team is the **mechanic**. Steve Matchett was a Formula 1 mechanic. He had to repair cars during the race. Now Steve works as a **sports commentator** on TV.

George Orwell was an important **writer**. Two of his most famous novels are called **Animal Farm** and **1984**. He was also a **journalist** and wrote for different newspapers. Before he started writing, he was a **police officer**.

Alexia Putellas is a Spanish **football player** and is one of the best in the world. She has won awards for her skills, including UEFA Women's Player of the Year Award, the Ballon d'Or Féminin and The Best FIFA Women's Player.

José Andrés is a famous **cook** who was born in Spain. He founded **World Central Kitchen**, which makes healthy food for people in countries going through difficult times.

Angelina Jolie is a famous **actor**. Her films include **Maleficent** and the **Kung Fu Panda** films. She also works to help people around the world. She loves planes, so she became a **pilot**, and she still enjoys flying now.

Shigeru Miyamoto designed the video games **Donkey Kong** and **Super Mario Bros**. When he was young, he studied art and wanted to be an **artist**, but then he discovered **Space Invaders** and he decided to become a **video game designer**.

2 **Read again and answer.**

1 Who is one of the most important people in a Formula 1 team?
2 What did Steve Matchett repair?
3 What are two of George Orwell's most famous novels?
4 What was George Orwell's job before he was a writer?
5 What did the football player win?
6 What did the cook do?
7 Who is a pilot and actor?
8 Which famous video games did Shigeru Miyamoto design?
9 Which two people help people in different countries?
10 How many of these people are on TV?

3 **Ask and answer.**

1 Which is the most exciting job? Why?

I think the game designer is the most exciting job because you can design games which you like to play!

2 Which job would you like to have? Why?

I'd like to be a cook, so that I can taste delicious food all day!

1 🎧 18 Listen and match. Say the job.

1 Good evening. This is Captain Bird speaking. Welcome aboard flight 241 from Dublin to London.

Pilot. That's 'e'.

a   b   c   d   e [1]   f

2 🎧 19 Listen again and choose the right words.

1 The plane is flying to **New York** / **London** / **Paris**.
2 The artist is painting **badly** / **quickly** / **carefully**.
3 The cook is making a **chocolate cake** / **carrot cake** / **cheesecake**.
4 Mr Hamilton can get his car at **ten o'clock** / **half past nine** / **half past ten**.
5 The designer is **happy** / **tired** / **hungry**.
6 The journalist is going to interview a **football player** / **swimmer** / **basketball player**.

3 Play the game. Guess it in ten.

Do you work at the fire station?   No, I don't.

Do you wear a uniform?   Yes, I do.

4 Read and think. Ask and answer.

What's William going to be when he grows up?   He's going to be a designer.

William	enjoys drawing and making things. He uses his computer to help him.
Teresa	likes writing and taking photos for her blog.
Katy	loves playing with cars and repairing things.
Richard	loves making cakes and working in the kitchen.
Robert	loves acting. He's in the drama club at school.
Helen	loves drawing and painting.

5 Think about someone you know who's got an interesting job. Answer the questions.

1 Who does this job?
2 What's his/her job?
3 What does he/she do at work?
4 Why do you think it's interesting?

6 📝 Write about an interesting job. Write 20–30 words.

Sounds and life skills
Thinking about the future

1 ▶ Watch the video. What jobs would they like to have when they are older?

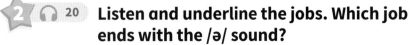

Pronunciation focus

2 🎧 20 Listen and underline the jobs. Which job ends with the /ə/ sound?

LENNY: Look at this … a nurse. That's an interesting job! I think I'm going to be a nurse when I'm older.

STELLA: Hmm, a nurse? That's great, Lenny. I think I'm going to be a dentist.

LENNY: A dentist? I thought that you always wanted to be a doctor?

STELLA: Maybe I can be a doctor and a dentist!

3 🎧 21 Listen and complete. Practise with a partner.

A: What _____ you going _____ be?

B: I think _____ going _____ be a _____ .

A: That's an interesting job.

4 Look at the job adverts. What kind of person do you need to be for these jobs?

Chefs wanted!

We are looking for chefs for two new restaurants in Rome.

You must be creative and speak Italian.

You must be good at making interesting pizzas and working very hard.

Email: Bella@Pizzaperfect.it

URGENT! Are you a ski instructor? Come and work at Winter Wonderland Ski Centre.

You must love snow and mountains! You must be patient and good at talking to people.

You must be good at skiing and snowboarding.

Email: sam.cold@WWSC.co.gp

Useful language

A chef must be creative.
A ski instructor must be good at talking to people.

5 In a group, discuss different jobs and what you need for them.

Diggory Bones

 1 **At what time is Diggory going to meet Brutus tomorrow? Why wasn't Brutus at the library?**

How can we stay safe?

1 🎧 **23** **Listen and read. Why is it important to control fire?**

How can we use fire?

People learnt how to make fire about a million years ago, and fire can be very useful.
We use it for cooking and for heat when we're cold. It also gives us light.

What causes fire?

Did you know fire needs three things: oxygen, fuel and heat? Oxygen is a gas, which is in the air all around us. Some examples of fuel are wood, coal, paper, gas and oil. When fuel gets very hot and mixes with oxygen, this can **start a fire**.

Not all fires are **man-made** and a fire can start **naturally**, like in a forest. It can also start **by accident**, for example, when cooking at home. It's important to control fire because it can **spread** quickly and it's very dangerous when it gets **out of control**.

How can we stop a fire?

Taking away the oxygen, fuel or heat means a fire can't burn any more. Water can **put out** a fire, but be careful: water can also start a fire if it has contact with electricity. So, never use water to put out a fire close to electrical equipment. Always use a **fire blanket** to cover the flames instead. This stops the oxygen and puts out the fire. Using **fire extinguishers** that spray foam is another way to stop the oxygen. A fire stops burning if there is no more fuel, so they sometimes **go out** on their own.

 2 **Read again and choose the correct options.**

1 Fire burns with _____ and _____ .
   a fuel   **b** heat   **c** foam
2 Fires can start _____ or _____ .
   a by accident   **b** without fuel **c** naturally
3 We use fire for _____ and _____ .
   a oxygen   **b** cooking   **c** heat
4 We can stop a fire with _____ or _____ .
   a water   **b** fuel   **c** a fire extinguisher
5 Fire is _____ and _____ .
   a easy to control **b** quick to spread **c** very hot

3 **How do you use fire safely in your daily lives?**

We have a BBQ in the garden that my parents use in the summer.

We have a fireplace with a metal grate in front for heating the living room in winter.

━ FIND **OUT MORE** ━
What are the main causes of house fires?

Read the safety leaflet. How many 'dos' and 'don'ts' are there?

DID YOU KNOW...?

Fire fighters have to get dressed in two minutes! The uniform is very heavy and made of special material to protect them from the heat.

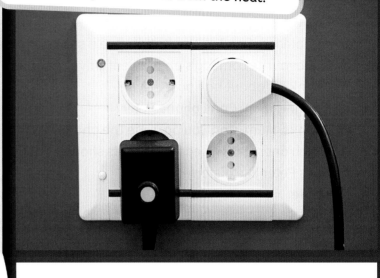

2

Fire safety

- ✗ Never play with matches, candles or other things that can start a fire.

- ✗ Don't put lots of plugs in electric sockets.

- ✓ It's important to have smoke alarms in your house.

- ✗ Never play near cookers, fireplaces or other areas where there is fire.

- ✓ Make sure you know the emergency phone number for the fire service.

- ✗ Never open any doors if there is fire on the other side.

- ✓ Go to a window and open it. Climb out if it's safe, or wait for help if you are upstairs.

Always remember the number to call in an emergency!

 Underline the imperatives with always and never in the safety leaflet in Activity 1.

 In pairs, discuss where safety advice is important. Write your ideas in your notebook.

Learning to write:
Imperatives with always and never

We use imperatives with **always** and **never** to show it is very important to do something.

Never use water to put out a fire near electrical equipment.

Always use a fire blanket to cover the flames.

Ready to write:

Go to Activity Book page 24.

Project

Make a poster about forest fire safety.

1 **Sarah is talking to her mother, Mrs Smith. Read the conversation and choose the best answer. You do not need to use all the letters.**

a Can we go out to the park?
b Yes, please. Can I phone Katy to see if she can come?
c My favourite comedy's on at twenty-five past five.
d I think it's about half past eleven.
e All right, then. Can I phone Peter?
f Thanks, Mum. Can you pass me the phone?
g Which ones shall I wear? My sports shoes?
h Does Peter like history?

Example

Mrs Smith: What time is it, Sarah?   Sarah: d

Questions

1 Mrs Smith: What do you want to do?
  Sarah: _____

2 Mrs Smith: OK. Put your shoes on.
  Sarah: _____

3 Mrs Smith: Yes, the blue ones. Listen, do you want to go with a friend?
  Sarah: _____

4 Mrs Smith: I think Katy's studying for an exam this afternoon.
  Sarah: _____

5 Mrs Smith: OK. Call him and see if he wants to come too.
  Sarah: _____
  Mrs Smith: Here you are. Tell Peter to bring his bike!

2 **Tell your partner the story.**   It's morning. The boy is going to school.

3 **Now write the story. Write 20–30 words.**

4 Play the game.

What are you going to do tomorrow?

Instructions: Go round the board. Say the time and what you are going to do at that time.
Think of a different activity for each time.
To keep playing you have to remember the activity which goes with each time. If you cannot
remember then go back to START and wait for another turn.

> That's quarter to seven. Tomorrow I'm going to wake up at quarter to seven.

> That's nine o'clock. Tomorrow I'm going to wake up at quarter to seven and go to school at nine o'clock.

3 City life

? Which places do you go to in your town or city?

 ▶ **Why are they going in the wrong direction? Watch and check.**

 ▶ **Watch again. Choose the right words.**

1 They arrive at **ten past two / twenty to three**.
2 They want information for their **blog post / school homework**.
3 They decide to visit a **bridge / museum** first.

4 They start outside a **shop / school**.
5 They're lost because of problems with the **map / bus**.
6 Tower Bridge is **behind / across** the street.

 Read and complete the sentences.

1 We have to go ⟶ this road.
2 We don't go across the river. We turn ↰ here.
3 Now we're at a ↰ .
4 We need to take the third street on the ↱ , then we walk ☐↑ this park.
5 Let's go ↖↑↗ .
6 It's just ⬆ the street.

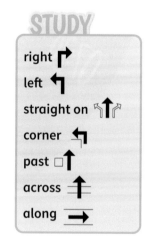

STUDY

right	↱
left	↰
straight on	↖↑↗
corner	↰
past	☐↑
across	⬆
along	⟶

 Ask and answer.

1 Why do you think Meera's dad said 'no phones'?
2 Do you know how to read a map? Are you good at following directions?

Language: directions and prepositions

1 ▶ **Can you remember the last lesson? Watch the language video.**

 2 **Look at the map. Read the directions and answer.**

1 Go along the High Street. Take the third street on the left and go across the river. What's on the right?

2 Go along the High Street and turn right into Blue Street. Turn left into Low Road and then go across Green Street. What's on the corner, on the left, opposite the music shop?

3 Go along the High Street and take the second street on the left. Walk past the playground. What's next to it?

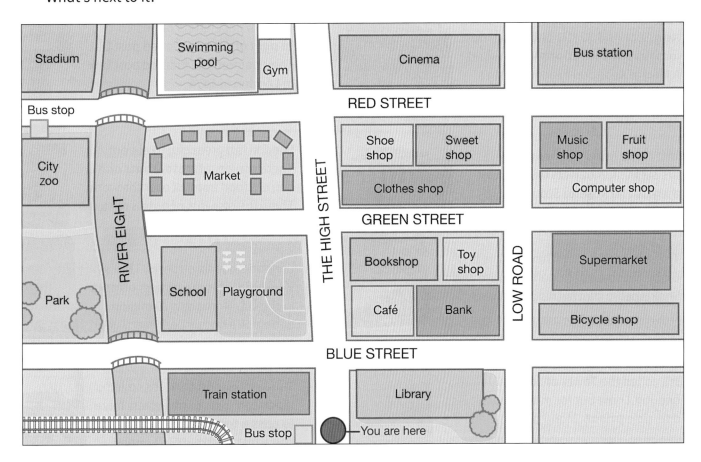

 3 🎧 24 **Listen to the directions and answer.**
🎧 **1** Go straight on. Take the second street on the left. What's at the end of the street?

 4 **Play the game.**
The river.

Go along the High Street and take the third street on the right. Go across Low Road and it's next to the music shop.

Is it the fruit shop? Yes, it is!

 5 📝 **Write the directions to (1) the bank and (2) the gym.**

Practice: directions and prepositions   29

1 Read the blog. Which is the busiest airport in the UK?

Kid's Box Reports

London is the capital city of England and the UK. Yesterday we went there and saw lots of interesting places. Here are some of our photos.

London

New Scotland Yard is one of the most famous **police stations** in the world. A king of Scotland lived in the first Scotland Yard.

NEW SCOTLAND YARD

You can post letters or postcards at **post offices** or in a red post box. They painted the first red post box in London in 1874.

POST OFFICE

This is the British **Museum**. There are six million objects here. One of them is The Rosetta Stone.

London is a great city to eat out. There are lots of **restaurants** and you can eat food from all over the world. There are also lots of **hotels** to stay in.

This is the new Globe **Theatre**. The first Globe Theatre was famous because William Shakespeare showed his plays there.

London's got six airports. This is Heathrow. It is the busiest **airport** in the UK. More than 70 million people use this airport every year!

This **castle** is next to Tower **Bridge**. It's called the Tower of London. It looks beautiful now but for many years it was a terrible **prison**. Many people died here.

This is a London **taxi**. It's called a black cab. Black-cab drivers have to pass a test to show that they know all the **streets** in London.

2 Read again and correct the sentences.

1 A king of England lived in the first Scotland Yard.
2 You can see The Rosetta Stone at the Natural History Museum.
3 Shakespeare showed his films at the Globe Theatre.
4 They painted the first London post box red in 1974.
5 London is a difficult place to eat out.
6 London's got seven airports.
7 The Tower of London was a post office for many years.
8 London buses are called black cabs.

3 Ask and answer.

1 Do you think London is an exciting city? Why?

> I think London is an exciting city because there's lots to see and do.

2 Where in London would you like to go? Why?

> I'd like to go the Globe Theatre to see a play.

1  25–26 Listen and complete. Listen and check. Then do karaoke.

bridge   castle   ~~museum~~   park   restaurant   station   street   taxi   theatre   zoo

Theatre, cinema,
Restaurant and hotel,
Museum, castle,
A story to tell.

I went to London,
To have a lovely day.
To go to a (1) museum and
The (2) _____ for a play.

I saw Tower (3) _____
And the (4) _____ too.
Walked in the (5) _____
And went to the (6) _____.

I went to a (7) _____
On the corner of the (8) _____.
I sat outside and
I had something to eat.

I took a (9) _____
Because it was late.
My train was in the (10) _____.
It was half past eight.

2 Ask and answer.

actor   bus driver   ~~cook~~   doctor   fire fighter   pilot   police officer   teacher

Who goes to work in a restaurant or hotel?   A cook.

3 Look at the map. Ask and answer.

Where's the museum?   It's between the gym and the library.

4 Think of a place you know. Give directions on how to get there from your school. Can your partner guess?

Go out of the door, turn left, take the second street on your right and walk past 'Flower's Restaurant'. What can you see?   Is it the stadium?   Yes, it is.

Sounds and life skills
Choosing options

1 ▶ Watch the video. Where are the young people and how do they feel?

Pronunciation focus

2 🎧 27 Listen. What do the circled words have in common?

STELLA: OK! Let's have a look at the map! How do we get there?

LENNY: We're (standing) outside a shop.

STELLA: So, we have to go (straight) along this (street). We don't go across the river. We turn left here at the (sports) shop. Let's go!

3 🎧 28 Listen and complete. Say the words. Can you think of more?

s t r eet, _____ aight
_____ and, _____ adium, _____ udy
_____ orts, _____ anish

4 In pairs, discuss the best places to visit in your town/city and why. Complete the table.

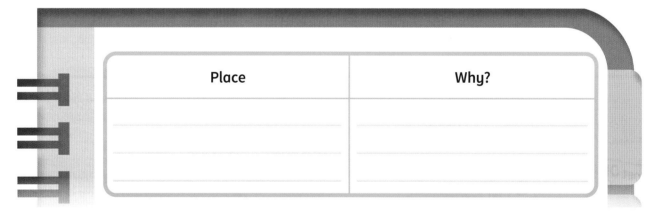

Place	Why?

5 In a group, choose one place to take a visitor to in your town/city.

Place _____

Where is it? _____

How can you get there? _____

What can you do there? _____

Useful language
Where shall we go?
… is the most famous.
How do we get there?

Diggory Bones

What does the letter mean?

It was the wrong library because it was the wrong city.

Which city does he mean?

I think he means the city of Alexandria in Egypt.

Of course! The library in Alexandria was the most important library in the ancient world.

What are we going to do now?

We're going to fly to Egypt.

Dad, we're going to Egypt. Can you take us to the airport, please?

Yes, son.

Outside the city of Alexandria there's a cave with secret writing on the walls.

And Brutus can use The Baloney Stone to understand the writing!

Now let's get a taxi and find a hotel ... Taxi!

What's in the cave, Dad?

People say the writing on the wall of the cave ...

... can open the door to mountains of secret treasure!

Brutus Grabbe!

 1 **Where was the most important library in the ancient world?**
Who was the taxi driver?

Story: unit language in context

What are the best modes of transport?

Want to hang out on the world's oldest elevated railway?

Then you must ride on Wuppertal's hanging train! It's a train where the cars 'hang' under the **tracks**. Every year more than 25 million passengers travel on this **public transport**, which opened in 1901. It's the easiest way to see this German city because you don't get **stuck in traffic**. It's electric too, so it's more **environmentally friendly** than travelling by car or bus.

Travel in the sky!

The city of Medellín in Colombia is built on lots of hills, so it's not the easiest place to get around. That's why they built the **cable car** system in 2004. Now it's the most popular form of public transport in the city! It's a fun way to travel and you get great city views. It doesn't cause **air or noise pollution**, so it's **greener** than buses and taxis.

Are you in a hurry?

The Shinkansen in Japan is the fastest **high-speed** rail system in the world. It uses the **newest technology** to give thousands of passengers a fast and comfortable ride every day. The Shinkansen's electric trains use less energy, so they cause less pollution than cars and planes. That's a great reason to use the country's high-speed **rail network**!

2 **Read again and complete the table.**

	Germany	Colombia	Japan
Type of transport	hanging train		
Advantage for passengers	You don't get stuck in traffic.		
How is it environmentally friendly?	It's electric.		

 3 **Which form of transport is your favourite and why? How do you like to travel around?**

> I think the best way to travel is on a cable car because there are great views.

> I like to travel around on trains because they're quicker than buses.

FIND OUT MORE
What are the most environmentally friendly modes of transport in your country?

1 **Read the advert. What are the advantages of using an e-scooter or e-bike?**

3

Public transport is getting greener

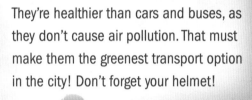

Public transport in our city is changing!

If you haven't got a car and the buses or underground trains are too overcrowded, why don't you use two wheels instead? Our e-scooters and e-bikes are the newest and easiest modes of transport in the city. Just download our app and get moving! You can travel on the road or in cycle lanes at a speed of up to 25 km/h. Our e-scooters and e-bikes are quicker than walking, which means they're the best choice when you're in a hurry.

They're healthier than cars and buses, as they don't cause air pollution. That must make them the greenest transport option in the city! Don't forget your helmet!

2 **Underline the superlatives and circle the comparatives in the advert in Activity 1.**

3 **In pairs, discuss modes of transport where you live. Write your ideas in your notebook.**

_____

_____

_____

Learning to write:

Comparatives and superlatives

We use comparatives to talk about two things.

They're **healthier than** cars and buses.

We use superlatives to talk about one thing from a group of the same things.

That must make them **the greenest** transport option in the city!

Ready to write:

Go to Activity Book page 34.

Project

Design a new, 'unusual' mode of transport.

4 Disaster!

? What kind of weather do you like or dislike?

 Why did the boat catch fire? Watch and check.

 Watch again. Order.

1 At first, it didn't work! But then he tried again.
2 Why didn't you go back to the beach?
3 Now we've got a new idea for our blog ... disasters!
4 We couldn't leave the island, so Dad had to phone for help!
5 Dad was listening to the radio. They said a storm was coming! [1]
6 We couldn't take any pictures – we were running away.

> **STUDY**
>
> **Were** you **listening** to the weather on the radio?
> We **weren't listening** to the radio.
> We **were listening** to music.

 Read and match.

1 They were getting warm	a lightning hit the boat.
2 The sky went dark	b because they were running away.
3 Lenny wasn't feeling very well	c when the journalist arrived.
4 When they were walking up the beach	d when they were sailing to the island.
5 They didn't get a picture of the fire	e so they were looking after him.

 Ask and answer.

1 How do you think each of the three children felt during the disaster?
2 How do you think they feel now? Why?

Can you remember the last lesson? Watch the language video.

 31–32 Read and guess. Listen and check. Then do karaoke.

climbing   eating   playing   sailing   sitting   skating   swimming   ~~walking~~

What were you doing when the storm began?
When the lightning hit and the water ran.
Where were you when the rain came down?
On the mountain, at the beach, in the forest or the town.

I was (1) __walking__ up the mountain,
He was (2) _____ over the lake,
We were (3) _____ in the park,
She was (4) _____ a piece of cake.
They were (5) _____ in the river,
He was (6) _____ on the sea,
She was (7) _____ up a wall,
I was (8) _____ under a tree.

 What were you doing when it happened? Write three sentences.

hurt my knee   dropped my mobile phone   lightning hit the tree   started to feel ill

teacher saw me   cut my hand   it started to rain   mother took a photo of me

 Play the game. Guess it in five.

I was having a picnic when it started to rain.

What was I doing when it started to rain?   Were you having a picnic?   Yes, I was.

 Choose one of your sentences and continue the story. Write 20–30 words.

1 What did you do?   2 What happened next?

1 Read the blog. How high was the wall of seawater in Messina?

ALL BLOGS   MY BLOG   NEW POST

Kid's Box
Reports

Disasters sometimes happen, as we recently found out. We decided to find out about some famous disasters.

Disasters

This ship is called the Titanic. On 14 April 1912 it was sailing across the Atlantic Ocean when it hit an **iceberg**. They couldn't see the iceberg because of the fog.

The Hindenburg was one of the biggest airships ever built. On 6 May 1937, when it was arriving in the USA, it caught fire. People think this happened because **lightning** hit it during a **storm**.

Hurricanes are very dangerous storms with strong winds. The worst Atlantic **hurricane** in history was the Great Hurricane in 1780, from 10–16 October.

When a **volcano** erupts, it throws hot liquid rock and gases into the air through the hole at the top. When Krakatoa erupted on 26 August 1883, it made the loudest sound ever heard.

On 1 November 1755 an earthquake hit Lisbon, in Portugal. The ground moved for ten minutes. The **earthquake** destroyed most of the buildings in the city.

On 28 December 1908, a **tsunami** hit Messina, in Italy. The enormous wall of seawater was about ten metres high. How high do you think the seawater is in this picture?

2 **Read again and correct the sentences.**

1 The Titanic hit an iceberg on 14 July 1912.
2 The Titanic was sailing across the Pacific Ocean.
3 The Hindenburg disaster was on 16 May 1937.
4 The Hindenburg airship was arriving in the UK.

5 The Great Hurricane was in 1870.
6 Krakatoa, the volcano, erupted on 28 August.
7 The Lisbon earthquake was on 1 November 1575.
8 The tsunami was on 28 October 1908.

3 **Ask and answer.**

1 Which do you think was the worst disaster? Why?

2 What was the worst weather you can remember? What were you doing?

> I think the earthquake was the worst disaster because the ground moved for ten minutes.

> I remember a hurricane. I was playing with my brother at home.

1 33 **Listen and repeat the chant.**

> January, February, March,
> April, May, June,
> July, August, September,
> October, November, December.

2 34 **Listen and say the months.**

> **1** It's sunny and windy. There are a lot of red apples on the trees …

> September.

January

February

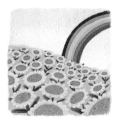
March

April

May

June

July

August

September

October

November

December

3 **Ask and answer.**

> It's February.

> What can you see?

> Some children are reading comics. They're sitting in their living room next to the fire.

4 **Cross out the extra word.**

1 What were they to doing on Wednesday 13 November?
2 There was a very bad storm on the 31 May.
3 They couldn't see because of was the fog.
4 Why was do he running?

5 The lightning hit many my car on 19 August.
6 My birthday was in the January.
7 The fire did started on 29 June.
8 In Antarctica there's a the lot of ice.

5 **Read the notes and write about what happened.**

Friday 13 March was a terrible day for Jane. What happened?
when / go downstairs / put / foot / on / toy car
fall down / break / leg
ambulance / come / take / to hospital
when / nurses / carry / Jane / into hospital / drop
now / Jane / in hospital / with / broken leg / and / broken arm

> When Jane was going downstairs, she put her foot on a toy car.

Sounds and life skills
Thinking creatively

1 ▶ Watch the video. When did the young people feel afraid, excited, sick and worried?

Pronunciation focus

2 🎧 35 Listen and write the circled words in the correct sound column in the table.

REPORTER: Why didn't (you) go back to the (beach)?

STELLA: Because (we) were very near the (island).
So we decided to (wait) there for the weather to get better.

LENNY: Yeah, we were walking up the beach to find somewhere (safe), when (lightning) hit the (boat) and it caught (fire)!

STELLA: We couldn't leave the island, so Dad had to (phone) for help!

A	E	I	O	U
sailing	sea	sky	hello	rescue

3 🎧 36 Listen and complete the rhyme with words from Activity 2.

There's a bad storm with rain and _____.
The _____'s on fire and it's very, very frightening.
Here comes the helicopter over the _____.
I hope it'll _____ my friends and me!

4 Look at the quiz in the magazine and write more questions.

Why didn't you ... ?

Are you good at thinking of reasons and excuses for not doing things? Do the quiz and find out.

● Why didn't you eat your breakfast?
● Why didn't you go to the park yesterday?
● Why didn't you come to class on time?

Why didn't you _____ ?
Why didn't you _____ ?

5 In pairs, ask and answer questions from the quiz. Can you think of interesting reasons?

Useful language

Why didn't you ...?
Because ...

Diggory Bones

 What terrible disaster happened in Ancient Alexandria? Why is it going to be very dark?

Story: unit language in context

41

Where can we find volcanoes?

1 🎧 38 **Listen and read. What causes volcanoes?**

www.planetwonderswow.com

Pacific Ring of Fire

Have you ever heard of Pompeii? On 24 August in the year 79, nearly 2,000 years ago, a nearby volcano called Vesuvius erupted and covered the city of Pompeii in rock and ash.

Vesuvius is in Italy, but did you know that there are volcanoes all over the world, and that one of the most active zones is the Pacific Ring of Fire? It's an area in the Pacific Ocean where there are almost 75% of the Earth's volcanoes.

The reason there are so many volcanoes in the Ring of Fire is because of tectonic plates, which are layers of rock just below the Earth's crust. The places where two plates meet are called plate boundaries, and when the plates move, which they do a lot, mountains and volcanoes form between them. Many of these plates meet at the Ring of Fire, which is why so many volcanoes appear in the area.

The movement of tectonic plates also causes earthquakes, and around 90% of these happen in the Pacific Ring of Fire.

One of the positive things that comes from the Pacific Ring of Fire is geothermal energy. Magma is the name of the very hot liquid rock that is deep underground. Around the Pacific Ring of Fire magma is very close to the Earth's crust, which makes it easier for engineers to use this heat from the ground as a source of green energy.

They can use this energy to heat houses, make hot water and even make electricity. Many countries, including the United States, Indonesia, Japan, New Zealand and the Philippines, already use geothermal energy.

2 **Read again and complete the diagram.**

tectonic plates   magma
the Earth's crust   plate boundary

1 _____

2 _____

3 _____

4 _____

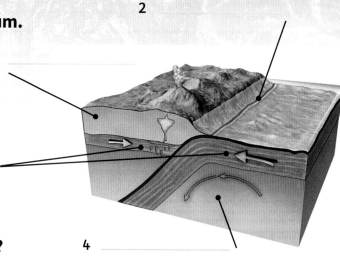

3 **Are there volcanoes in your country?**
Are they active, dormant or extinct?
What other volcanoes do you know about?

> There are a lot of volcanoes in my country but they're all dormant.

> I know about Mount Saint Helens, which is an active volcano in the United States.

— FIND **OUT** MORE —
What is the largest volcanic eruption in history?

1 Read the message. What is Iceland famous for?

DID YOU KNOW...?

The largest volcano in the world is Mauna Loa in Hawaii. At 9,159 metres high, it is bigger than Mount Everest. However, 5,000 metres of that is underwater!

To: Petra
Subject: Iceland is amazing!

Hi Petra,

During the summer holiday, I visited the amazing island of Iceland. Iceland is a volcanic island in the North Atlantic Ocean, which is famous for its dramatic geography.

In Iceland, you can see geysers, which are holes in the ground that blast out jets of water and steam. There are also natural hot springs, huge lava fields and glaciers. In fact, glaciers cover 10% of the island. Sometimes there are volcanic eruptions and I learnt that, back in 2010, a volcano erupted and filled the sky with ash. It meant that all planes in about 20 countries couldn't take off!

Iceland uses its interesting geography to make electricity. In fact, the island makes electricity by using power from its rivers and waterfalls and heat from the ground, which is very good for the environment.

I hope I can go back to Iceland again one day because it is a fantastic place. I'll tell you more about my trip when I see you!

Bye for now,

Eric

---

2 Underline **which** to give extra information in the message in Activity 1.

Learning to write:

Which to give extra information

We can use **which** to give extra information.

> The reason there are so many volcanoes in the Ring of Fire is because of tectonic plates, **which** are layers of rock just below the Earth's crust.

3 In pairs, discuss places you know that are famous for their landscape. Write your ideas in your notebook.

Ready to write:

Go to Activity Book page 42.

Project

Make a presentation on a volcanic eruption.

Review Units 3 and 4

1 **Read the letter and write the missing words.**

Dear Aunt Anika,

I'm writing to tell you about the great time we had last weekend.
I think Mum told you we were going to Manchester on Saturday.
Well, we went to the stadium to see a football game, because
Manchester United were playing against Liverpool. I really
enjoyed it but, sadly, Liverpool didn't (1)_____ .
They (2)_____ 1–0.
On Sunday we spent the day exploring the city.
We got lost because we didn't have a (3)_____ .
No problem! We asked a police officer for (4)_____ and he showed us where to go.
We visited the Lowry Museum which had some interesting paintings by a famous
(5)_____ from Manchester, L S Lowry. There is a picture of the museum attached to
this email. Hope you like it.

Yours,

Jamie

2 **39** **Listen and write. There is one example.**

1 Who was he visiting: grandad

2 Where did they go first: _____

3 Address: _____ Road

4 Opening times: From 10:00 to _____

5 Where they had lunch: _____

6 Transport home: _____

3 Play the game.

Find your way home

Instructions: Go round the board following the instructions. When you stop on a picture, spell the word. If it's right, roll again. If it's wrong, stop.

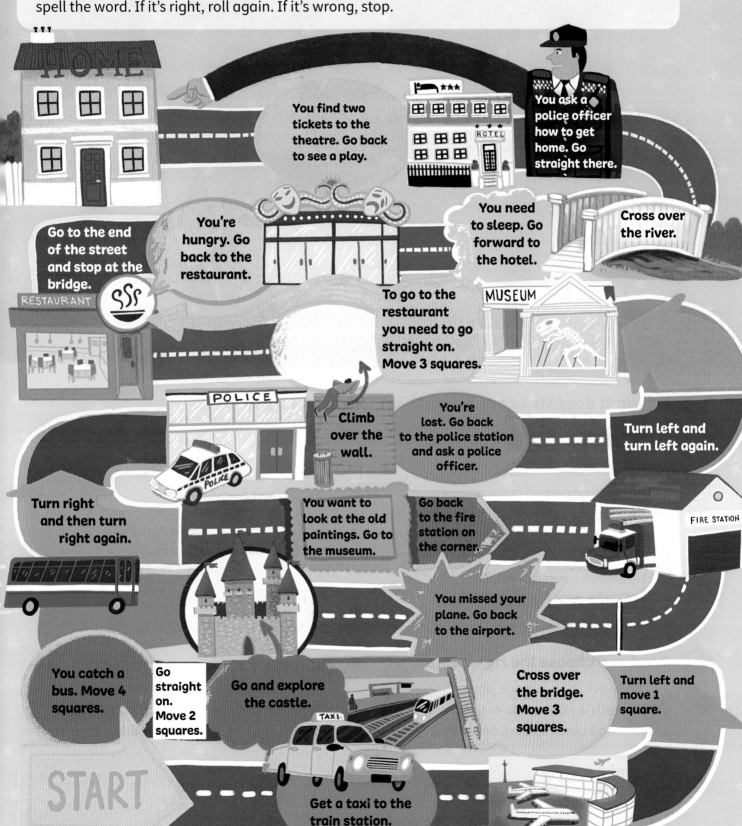

5 Material things

JOKE SHOP

 1 ▶ **What does Stella put her teeth in? Watch and check.**

 2 ▶ **Watch again. Say 'yes' or 'no'.**

1 The sweet shop is made of brick.   Yes.
2 The children go to a pet shop.
3 The eggs are made of fur.
4 Meera wants to buy some toys.
5 The teeth are made of sugar.
6 The snakes are made of paper.
7 The spiders are made of rubber.
8 Stella's afraid of spiders.

STUDY

The eggs **are made of** white chocolate.
The spider **isn't made of** fur.
What **are** they **made of**?

 3 Read and choose the right words.

1 The sweet shop is made **on / of** brick.
2 The teeth **is / are** made of sugar.
3 The small black spiders are **made / make** of fur.

4 The eggs **is / are** made of white chocolate.
5 The snake is made of **rubber / stone**.
6 The spider on Stella's shoulder **is / isn't** real.

 4 Ask and answer.

1 What did you think of Meera and Lenny's joke with the spider?
2 Look around your classroom. What are things made of?

1 ▶ **Can you remember the last lesson? Watch the language video.**

2 **Ask and answer.**

> **a** What's the school made of?

> I think it's made of stone.

 a
 b
 c
 d

 e
 f
 g
 h

3 🎧 40 **Listen and check.**

> 🎧 **1** Is your new schoolbag made of leather?

> Yes, it is.

> That's 'c'.

4 **Read and match.**

1 This is my favourite hat. I can wear it every day because it changes with the weather. When it's raining, it's got two pieces of plastic to cover my ears. ☐ c

2 When it's cold, a special scarf, which is made of fur, comes out to cover my neck. ☐

3 When it's sunny, my hat protects me from the sun. I've got some sunglasses made of special plastic to protect my eyes. ☐

4 These are my favourite shoes. I wear them at the weekend. They are purple. ☐

5 I don't need to wear socks with my new shoes. They keep me cool in the summer. They're blue. Look! ☐

6 If I jump or drop the shoes on the floor, they bounce. The shoes can help me to jump very high – up to two metres! This is because they are made of a special rubber called 'bounce-a-lot'. I'm going to bounce to the park. Goodbye. ☐

 a
 b
 c
 d
 e
 f

5 **Read again and correct the sentences.**

1 The hat changes every day.
2 When it's raining, it's got two pieces of plastic to cover his eyes.
3 The sunglasses are made of special rocks.
4 The shoes can help her swim.
5 If you drop the shoes, they dance.
6 The shoes are made of wood.

Read the blog. What's the most important material? Why?

ALL BLOGS   MY BLOG   NEW POST

Kid's Box Reports

Materials can be man-made or natural. We make man-made materials in factories. We get natural materials from rocks in the ground, animals or plants. Here are some interesting things made of different materials.

Materials

Most houses are made of **bricks**, **stone** or **wood**, but Edouard Arsenault used 12,000 **glass** bottles to build this amazing house.

Card and **paper** come from trees. Card is stronger than paper. This tower is made of thin **card** and the bridge is made of paper.

Gold and silver are precious metals. This car is made of 80 kilograms of gold and 15 kilograms of **silver**. The tyres aren't made of **metal**, but you have to drive it very carefully!

Most animals have **fur**, but sheep have **wool**. We use wool to make fabric for clothes. We can also make things at home from wool. Look at these beautiful cushions. The covers are made of wool.

Lots of things are made of **plastic**. Today we use plastic more than any other material in the world. We must recycle plastic. 'Recycle' means use it again in a different form. This bottle of shampoo is made of recycled plastic.

 Read again and answer.

1 Where do we make man-made materials?
2 What are most houses made of?
3 How many glass bottles did Arsenault use to build his house?
4 How much gold is in the car?

5 Where do card and paper come from?
6 Where does wool come from?
7 What are the cushion covers made of?
8 What does 'recycle' mean?

 Choose five materials. Tell your partner about things made of these materials.

My book is made of paper and card.

Read and choose the right words.

1 Paper and card are made of **wood** / **leather** / **metal**.
2 Gold comes from **animals** / **the ground** / **trees**.
3 Wood comes from **the ground** / **trees** / **flowers**.
4 Fur comes from **trees** / **sand** / **animals**.
5 Glass is made of **leaves** / **sand** / **wood**.
6 Wool comes from a **sheep** / **cow** / **bear**.

2 🎧 ▶ 41–42 **Listen and order. Listen and check. Then do karaoke.**

a This table's made of wood,
And that skirt's made of grass. ☐

b From rocks, plants or animals,
Or from a factory. ☐

c This scarf is made of wool,
And I wear it when it's cold. ☐

d This chair is made of metal,
That bowl is made of glass. ☐

e Some things are made of plastic,
Which can be strong and hard. ☐

f This box is made of silver,
That watch is made of gold. ☐

g Everything's material,
Everything we see. 1

h Books are made of paper,
Their covers are made of card. ☐

3 **Close your book. What can you remember from the song?**

What's the bowl made of?   It's made of glass.

 Look around your classroom. Find and write two things for each material.

wood	metal	glass	plastic	paper
pencil				

  What are things made of in your classroom? Write 20–30 words.

Sounds and life skills

Talking about different ideas

1 ▶ Watch the video. Which shops do they go in?

Pronunciation focus

2 🎧 43 **Read and listen. What happens to the last sound in the first word in blue?**

MEERA: Ooh – look at this sweet shop! It's fantastic!
STELLA: Yeah, and it's all made of brick.
LENNY: Come on Stella!
STELLA: In a minute!

3 🎧 44 **Listen and complete. Practise with a partner.**

1 Come _____ .
2 Look _____ !
3 Look _____ this.

4 You're _____ star.
5 I've got _____ great idea.
6 _____ a minute.

4 🎧 45 **Look at the game. Listen to young people playing it and tick (✓) the phrases they use.**

The yes/no game

a soft toy car

a toy car

a skateboard

a bicycle

a tablet

a drawing book

a magnifying glass

a cup

Is it big? ☐
Is it long? ☐
Is it made of wood? ☐
Is it made of paper? ☐
Is it made of metal? ☐
Has it got legs? ☐
Has it got pages? ☐
Do you use it to play? ☐
Do you use it to learn? ☐

Wait a minute. ☐   You're a star! ☐   Come on. ☐
Nice one! ☐   Look at this. ☐

Useful language

Is it made of …?
Has it got …?
Do you use it to …?

5 **In pairs, play the game.**

Diggory Bones

 1 Where was Brutus carrying The Baloney Stone? Which two materials are the different bowls made of?

Story: unit language in context

What can you make with recycled materials?

1 🎧 **47** **Listen and read. What materials do they use?**

Giant Tap, Switzerland

I saw this amazing **sculpture** in a park in Winterthur. It looks like a tap is **magically** hanging in the air, but it's actually a simple **illusion**. Water from under the ground travels up a pipe, which holds the giant metal tap in place. We can't see it because the water flows over it when it comes out.

Everyone stops to look at it **carefully** to see how it works. It feels magical, and that's the idea of art – to create something different that surprises us.

The Bruges Whale, Belgium

This giant whale is made of **plastic waste** from the Pacific Ocean and when you look **closely**, you can see that there are thousands of **plastic objects**, from bins to toilet seats! Two **artists** created the sculpture to show how much we're polluting our world. Did you know there's more plastic in our oceans than whales!

Lots of artists are working with **recycled materials** now, which is important because it connects art with the world around us. I love how creative and interesting this sculpture is.

Puppy, Spain

This huge dog sculpture sits outside a museum in Bilbao. It's very special because it's **completely** covered in plants – about 38,000 flowers in total! Metal pipes **inside** a **hidden** frame send water to the plants to keep them alive.

I love that the **sculptor** uses nature because it shows that art is always growing and changing. The artist wanted to create something to make people happy, and I think this sculpture really does that.

2 **Read again and complete the table.**

	Giant Tap	The Bruges Whale	Puppy
What is it made of?	metal, (1) _____ water _____	recycled (4) _____	metal (7) _____ , (8) _____
How was it made?	Water travels up a (2) _____ and flows out of the tap.	The artists collected plastic (5) _____ from the Pacific Ocean.	Water travels through pipes to keep the (9) _____ alive.
What is the message?	It shows that art can (3) _____ us.	It gives the message that we're (6) _____ our world.	Art is (10) _____ and (11) _____ .

3 **How do the sculptures make you feel and why? What other sculptures do you know about?**

> This sculpture makes me laugh.

> I saw a metal sculpture of a bear and a tree in the centre of Madrid.

FIND OUT MORE

What is the biggest sculpture in the world?

Art: sculptures | 🛡 creative thinking

1 Read the review. What message does the artist want to give?

DID YOU KNOW…?
At nearly 55 metres tall and 25 metres wide, the Portrait of Decebalus is the biggest sculpture in Europe!

Domestic towers

I saw some amazing sculptures in Germany last week. They are 'Domestic towers' and I liked them because they are actually three sculptures in one.

There are three towers painted brightly and each one is cleverly made with household objects.

The green tower is made of recycled objects you find in gardens, and there's a plant pot at the centre with a flower growing in it. The blue tower is made of tools, paint pots and other things you might find in your garage.

The red tower is my favourite because each time I look at it, I see something new.

There are tyres, boxes, sports equipment, a keyboard and a video camera. There's even a bike at the top!

I love the way the artist skilfully linked all the objects together. It shows we can be creative because we can make something beautiful from everyday objects or rubbish.

2 Underline the adverbs in the review in Activity 1.

3 In pairs, discuss a sculpture or statue that you like. Compare the materials used in each one. Write your ideas in your notebook.

Sculpture	Materials

Learning to write:
Adverbs
We use adverbs to describe how we do something.
  It looks like a tap is **magically** hanging in the air.
  It's **completely** covered in plants.

Ready to write:
Go to Activity Book page 52.

Project
Make or draw a sculpture out of recycled materials.

6 Senses

Touch

1 ▶ **What do they want to make for their next blog post? Watch and check.**

2 ▶ **Watch again. Order.**

1 It smells like Lenny's socks.
2 What does it feel like?
3 It tastes like pineapple.
4 It sounds like someone's falling down the stairs.
5 What does this taste like, Lenny?
6 In this week's science club we're going to look at the five senses.
7 What does this smell like, Stella?
8 It's very soft. It feels like fur.

> **STUDY**
>
> What does it **look / feel / taste / smell / sound like?**
>
> It **looks / feels / tastes / smells / sounds like** coffee.

(order box marked: 6 → 1)

3 **Read and order the words.**

1 a / lorry. / sounds / My / car / like
_____

2 feels / like / His / jacket / fur.
_____

3 does / taste / What / like? / that / soup
_____

4 our / mother / look / Who / like? / does
_____

4 **Ask and answer.**

1 How did the kids explore their senses? Which was your favourite?

2 Talk about your family. Who do you look like?

1 **Can you remember the last lesson? Watch the language video.**

2 **48 Listen. What does it sound like?**

 1. It sounds like a car.

3 **Play the game. What does it sound like?**

- Think of five things which make different sounds.
- Write the words on five small pieces of paper.
- Give your pieces of paper to your teacher.

- Play the game with the class.
- Make the sounds and guess.
- Now play the game in groups.

Tick tock tick tock.   It sounds like a clock.

4 **Ask and answer. What does it look like?**

What do you think number 1 looks like?   I think it looks like a cat's nose.   So do I.

5 **Ask and answer. What does it feel like?**

What does number 1 feel like?   It feels soft and furry.

1 **Read the blog. What ingredients would you put on your pizza?**

ALL BLOGS   MY BLOG   NEW POST

Kid's Box Reports

We wanted to learn how to make pizza, so we went to Luigi's Italian restaurant and spoke to Mario, the cook. Before we started, we washed our hands.

Making pizza

First we made the base. The base is made of **dough**. We put some flour, **yeast**, salt and water into a **bowl** and **mixed** them well. Then we left the dough for an hour so it could grow.

Then we put tomato, cheese, salami sausage, olives and onion on top of the base. After that we added some black pepper and cooked it in the **oven** for 15 minutes.

When it was ready, we put the pizza onto a **plate**. Mario uses special plates in the restaurant. They're very big and they're made of wood.

You can eat pizza with your hands, but you need to **cut** it with a **knife** first. This one is round but pizzas can also be square.

We had the pizza with salad. We used a big **spoon** and **fork** to mix it. Here's a picture of our delicious meal. It looks good, but it tasted even better!

2 **Read again and correct the sentences.**

1 Before they started, they washed their feet.
2 Pizza base is made of rubber.
3 They put some flour, yeast, salt and milk into a bowl.
4 They put some black chocolate on top of the pizza.
5 They cooked the pizza in the oven for 25 minutes.
6 The plates are very big and they're made of glass.
7 Mario used a spoon to cut the pizza.
8 They mixed the salad with a knife and fork.

3 **Talk about your favourite meal. Tell your partner which ingredients you need.**

My favourite meal is pasta Bolognese. I need pasta, water, tomatoes, meat and onions.

 **49–50** **Read and match. Listen and check. Then do karaoke.**

My name's Mario,
I'm an Italian cook.
If you want to make a pizza,
Then listen to me and look. | e |

Take salt, yeast, flour and water,
Put them in a bowl.
Mix them all together,
And wait for it to grow. | |

When the base is bigger,
Throw it in the air.
Use your hands to turn it,
Don't get it in your hair. | |

Now you choose your topping,
Tomato, pepper and cheese.
You can choose anything,
Sausage, onion and meat. | |

Cook for 15 minutes,
Then put it on a plate.
Cut it with a knife and fork,
Mmm. Now that tastes great! | |

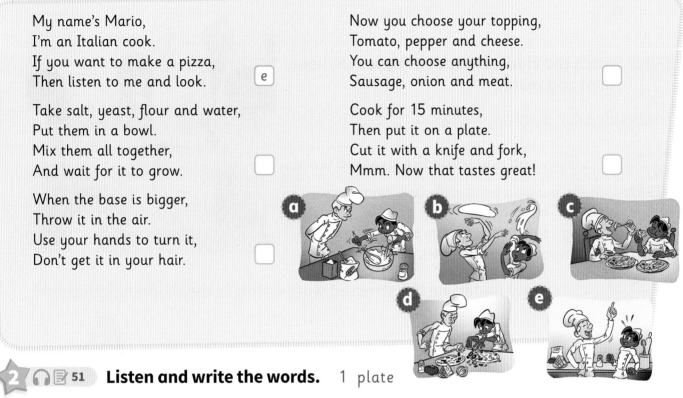

2 **51** **Listen and write the words.** 1 plate

3 **Read and complete. Write the recipe in your notebook.**

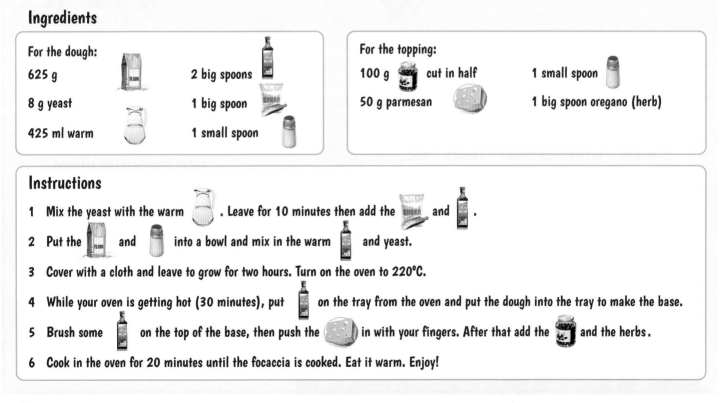

Ingredients

For the dough:
625 g
8 g yeast
425 ml warm

2 big spoons
1 big spoon
1 small spoon

For the topping:
100 g   cut in half
50 g parmesan

1 small spoon
1 big spoon oregano (herb)

Instructions

1 Mix the yeast with the warm   . Leave for 10 minutes then add the   and   .

2 Put the   and   into a bowl and mix in the warm   and yeast.

3 Cover with a cloth and leave to grow for two hours. Turn on the oven to 220°C.

4 While your oven is getting hot (30 minutes), put   on the tray from the oven and put the dough into the tray to make the base.

5 Brush some   on the top of the base, then push the   in with your fingers. After that add the   and the herbs.

6 Cook in the oven for 20 minutes until the focaccia is cooked. Eat it warm. Enjoy!

4 **Think about your favourite meal. Write a shopping list of the ingredients.**

▶ **Watch the video. What do they touch, hear, smell and taste?**

Touch

Pronunciation focus

 🎧 52 **Listen and underline the stressed words.**

MEERA: Stella, put your hand in the box. What does it feel like?

STELLA: It's very soft. It feels like fur. Is it an animal?

LENNY: No, Stella. It's my toy spider.

3 🎧 53 **Listen and underline the stressed words. How is the meaning different?**

1 This is my toy spider.

2 This is my toy spider.

3 This is my toy spider.

4 This is my toy spider.

4 🎧 54 **Complete the senses poem with the words in the box. Listen and check.**

birds   light   shower   toast   toothpaste

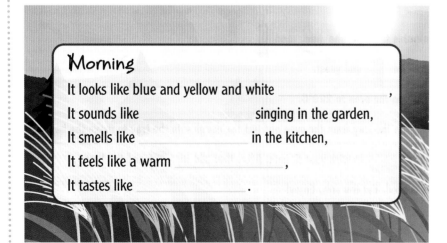

Morning

It looks like blue and yellow and white _____ ,
It sounds like _____ singing in the garden,
It smells like _____ in the kitchen,
It feels like a warm _____ ,
It tastes like _____ .

5 📝 **In pairs, write a senses poem about a season, time of year, time of day or a favourite place.**

Useful language
What does it … like?
It … like …

1 **What's a snake bowl? What does Diggory use to get Brutus out?**

How do we make noises?

THE SCIENCE OF SOUND

Sounds are created when objects **vibrate**. And these **vibrations** are called **sound waves**. We can't see them, but they travel through the air until they reach our ears, and we hear them as sounds.

If we shake a tiny bell, it vibrates quickly, so we hear a high ring in our ears. If we hit a large bell, the sound waves are stronger and vibrate more slowly, so we hear a low sound.

Some sounds can be high but very loud. Did you know that a baby's cry is louder than the honk of a car horn? However, the loudest sound on Earth is low and loud – it's the sound of a volcano erupting!

Sound needs to travel through something, like an object or air or water. If there is no air, like in space, there is no sound! Wind is air but it has no sound. It's the wind blowing against an object that makes the sound.

Sound travels four times faster through water than air so it can travel further through water. That's how whales can hear each other even when they are hundreds of kilometres apart!

2 Read again and choose the correct words.

1 Vibrations of sound are called sound _____.   a energy   b waves

2 Fast vibrations make a _____ sound.   a high   b low

3 Slow vibrations make a _____ sound.   a low   b high

4 Sound needs to travel through something, like _____ or water.   a air   b space

5 Wind makes sound when it blows against _____.   a objects   b air

6 In water, sound travels _____ than in air.   a faster   b slower

3 Close your eyes and listen. What can you hear? What sounds do you like and dislike?

I can hear traffic outside the school. I don't like it because it's too noisy.

I can hear myself breathing. I like it because it relaxes me.

— FIND **OUT MORE** —
What is the maximum speed of sound?

1 🎧 **57** **Read and listen to the poem. Which sound doesn't the writer like?**

Sounds I love to hear

I love to hear my cat meowing because it means she wants me to cuddle her.

I love to hear the 'ding-dong' of the doorbell ringing because it means we have a visitor.

I love to hear my friends giggling because it means they are happy and having fun.

I love to hear plates clattering in the kitchen because it means dinner will be ready soon.

I love to hear rain tapping on my window because it makes me feel cosy and safe inside.

But I hate to hear the cars zooming outside because it makes me feel stressed.

2 **Underline the sound words in the poem in Activity 1.**

Learning to write:

Sound words

We use sound words to help the reader hear the sounds you are writing about.

If we shake a tiny bell, we hear a high **ring**.

A baby's cry is louder than the **honk** of a car horn.

3 📝 **In pairs, brainstorm sounds that you love and sounds that you hate. Explain why. Complete the table in your notebook.**

Sounds I love	Sounds I hate

Ready to write:

Go to Activity Book page 60.

Project

Make a poster about your favourite sounds.

Review Units 5 and 6

1 **Read the text. Choose the right words from the table and write them on the lines.**

Wall | Find friends | Chat | Profile

Hi all,
Here are a few lines to tell you about (1) _____ our _____
football team. We're (2) _____ the Cambridge
Flyers. We (3) _____ indoor football at the
weekends and we play against other teams from towns
near ours. There (4) _____ seven of us in the
team. We always change players (5) _____
only five can play at a time. (6) _____ week we
played against the team from Oldcastle. They played
really (7) _____ and they won 4–1.
We (8) _____ the first goal but then they scored
the next four. We're going to win our next game though.
That's all for now,
Li Wei

1	our	we	us
2	called	calling	call
3	plays	playing	play
4	is	am	are
5	but	because	so
6	Next	Every	Last
7	well	good	beautiful
8	marked	scored	do

2 🎧 58 **Listen and tick (✓) the box.**

1 When is David's birthday?

January February March

A ✓   B ☐   C ☐

2 What is he going to do on Saturday?

A ☐   B ☐   C ☐

3 What time is the party?

A ☐   B ☐   C ☐

4 Where are they going to go?
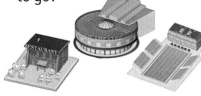

A ☐   B ☐   C ☐

5 What was his favourite present last year?

A ☐   B ☐   C ☐

6 What would he like to get this year?

A ☐   B ☐   C ☐

3 Play the game.

Collect the materials

Instructions: The winner is the first person to get seven things made of different materials.
Roll the dice and move your counter. Say what you can see and what it's made of. If you're right, have another turn. If you're wrong, stop.
If you stop on something made of a material which you've got, miss a turn.

FINISH

START

7 Natural world

1 ▶ **Why are they picking up rubbish? Watch and check.**

2 ▶ **Watch again. Say 'yes' or 'no'.**

1 They've got five days to write their next blog post. *No.*
2 Stella thinks they should put some sun cream on.
3 A woman's taking glass bottles and plastic bags out of the lake.
4 She has to do this every day.
5 People should look for a recycling bin.
6 The kids shouldn't tell their friends about the problem.

> **STUDY**
>
> People **should take** their rubbish with them.
> They **shouldn't leave** it on the grass.
> What **should** we **do** about this?

3 **Read and match.**

1 It's very hot	a do to help?
2 When the sun is strong	b our rubbish on the grass.
3 We shouldn't leave	c rubbish into lakes or rivers.
4 We should always	d clean up after a picnic in the countryside.
5 We shouldn't throw our	e so we should put our hats on.
6 What should we	f we should use sun cream.

4 **Ask and answer.**

1 Why was the woman cleaning the lake?
2 What do you do with your rubbish when you're outside?

1 ▶ **Can you remember the last lesson? Watch the language video.**

 2 **Read the posts and choose the right words. Who do you agree with? Why?**

 How can we help look after our world?

Plastic isn't good for the planet. We **(1) should / shouldn't** stop using plastic. It can take 1,000 years to disappear and we are filling the whole Earth with ugly, terrible, dirty plastic. It's a disaster! We really **(2) should / shouldn't** buy plastic bags or plastic bottles.

Oliver, 13

There is water all around us – in fact more than 70% of the Earth is water. We **(3) should / shouldn't** decide how to use water as carefully as we can, so that in the future we have water to drink, cook and wash our clothes. Everyone **(4) should / shouldn't** remember to turn off taps and have short showers instead of baths.

Pablo, 11

We use energy for everything, from computer games to playing the electric guitar, but making it causes pollution. So, you **(5) should / shouldn't** remember to turn everything off when you finish playing and save energy.

Maria, 12

Did you know that every year we throw away more than a billion tonnes of food? That's frightening! You **(6) should / shouldn't** try to prepare only the food that you need. If you have any food left, you can share it with your friends.

Li Jing, 12

3 **Read the questions and write the name.**

1 Who thinks that we can save food and be kind to others? _____
2 Who thinks that we need a plan for the future? _____
3 Who thinks that something we use takes a long time to disappear? _____
4 Who thinks that we need to do something very important after we have fun? _____

4 🎧 ▶ 59–60 **Read and guess. Listen and check. Then do karaoke.**

clean   climb   ~~drop~~   go   jump   put   run   stop   walk

You shouldn't ___drop___ your rubbish,
You should _____ it in a bin.
You shouldn't leave it on the ground,
You should _____ up everything.
Here comes the bear, here comes the bear!
It's coming for your tea!

Should I move or should I _____?
Should I _____ that tree?
I should do something now.
That bear / cow is after me.

You shouldn't _____ across the field,
You should _____ around.
You shouldn't go too near that cow,
It can push you to the ground.
You should _____ ...
You should _____ quickly!

 5 📝 **How do you think we should look after our world? Write 20–30 words.**

1 Read the blog. Which animal fact is the most interesting for you?

ALL BLOGS   MY BLOG   NEW POST

Kid's Box Reports

There are more than 15,000 endangered species of animals and birds, and even more species of insects in danger, like butterflies. Let's take a look at what people are doing to protect them so that they do not become extinct.

Nature watch

There are two special National Parks in Siberia to protect Siberian tigers from people who want to catch them for their beautiful striped fur.

Tigers are famous for their stripes. They are an endangered species and we should protect them. When we protect tigers, we protect forests which give people around the world clean air, water, food and materials. Another animal famous for its stripes is the mountain zebra. Thanks to conservation projects, mountain zebras are now safe from extinction.

The Lost Ladybug Project asks people to take photos of this beetle, or ladybird, if they see it and post them online.

This is the nine-spotted lady beetle. It has four black spots on each wing and one in the middle of its body. It lives in North America and it is an endangered species.

Did you know that the last day of April every year is **Save the Frogs Day**? There are educational events in more than 56 countries.

Frogs are in danger all over the world. The frog in the picture is Lehmann's poison frog. It is found in Colombia. It has red, orange or yellow stripes.

Let's celebrate beautiful butterflies! Every two years there's a **Butterfly Beauty Festival** in Asia from November to March. This helps us to protect the butterflies and learn more about them.

Butterflies are beautiful, flying insects. This butterfly is a purple spotted butterfly. It has white spots on its purple wings. Every year millions of butterflies fly to a different place to escape cold weather. This can be dangerous, so we need to protect them.

2 Read again and answer.

1 How many endangered species are there?
2 How do the special parks in Siberia protect the tigers?
3 When we protect tigers, what else do we protect?
4 Which animal has a spotted body and wings?
5 Where does the Lehmann's poison frog live?
6 Which animal has red, orange or yellow stripes?
7 When is the **Butterfly Beauty Festival**?
8 Which animal has got white spots on its wings?

3 Ask and answer.

1 Which animals would you like to protect? Why?
2 What should we do to protect this animal? Think of a class project.

1 Look at the pictures. Describe them to your partner.

Queen Alexandra's birdwing butterfly.

Male

Female

> The female is brown.

> The male is more beautiful than the female.

2   61 Listen. Write words or numbers.

MARY'S PROJECT

Name of butterfly	1	Queen Alexandra's
Wings measure (Male)	2	cm
Wings measure (Female)	3	cm
Description (Female)	4	
Description (Male)	5	

3 Read and complete.

butterflies   extinct   garden   should   ~~thousands~~   trees

Help endangered species

There are **(1)** _thousands_ of endangered species in the world. Endangered means there is time to help them before they disappear.

They are not **(2)** _____. So, what should we do? We **(3)** _____ look after our world and ask everyone to help make it a cleaner place for animals and insects to live in. We should make oceans, ponds, streams and the air much cleaner than they are now … and you can help too!

You can:
- help clean and protect the habitat in your **(4)** _____, near your house or on your school ground.
- plant **(5)** _____ and flowers where insects like **(6)** _____ can live.
- help projects to plant riverbanks with plants which make the ground stronger and give animals a habitat.

4 Look at the pictures. Talk about what you should do.

> I think we should recycle all bottles.

> Yes, I agree.

a

b

c

d

e

f

Sounds and life skills

Taking care of your community

 1 ▶ **Watch the video. Where are the young people and how do they feel?**

Pronunciation focus

 2 🎧 62 **Listen and underline the stressed words.**

MEERA: People shouldn't leave their rubbish on the grass or throw it in the lake.

LENNY: So, what should they do with it?

PARK RANGER: They should look for a recycling bin or take their rubbish home with them.

 3 **Think and write. Practise with a partner.**

A: People shouldn't _____ .

B: What should they do?

A: They should _____ .

 4 **Read the flyer. What information does it give?**

Let's clean it up!
Here's how to organise your own neighbourhood clean-up.

Get permission Ask your family for permission to do a clean-up in your neighbourhood. Ask an adult to help you.

Decide where Think about where you want to pick up rubbish. Is there a park or a beach near you that needs help?

Get help Find friends and family to join the clean-up. The more people, the better! Ask local shops or your local council if they can give you free rubbish bags, gloves or tools.

Take pictures On the day of the clean-up, take lots of pictures that you can share afterwards.

Say thank you Thank everyone for their help.

NOTES: OUR NEIGHBOURHOOD CLEAN-UP

Where	
When	
Who should we ask for help?	
Who should take photos?	

 5 **In a group, plan your own neighbourhood clean-up and make notes.**

 Why should they climb the ladder slowly and carefully? What do the butterflies look like?

Story: unit language in context

69

How can we help endangered species?

1 🎧 64 **Listen and read. Why are these animals endangered?**

Turtle

I joined the **Turtle Protection Project** two years ago. Turtles come to our beach each year to lay their eggs, but they are an **endangered species**. Humans are a big problem because they catch turtles to sell their eggs, meat and shells.

The project teaches people why we should **protect** turtles, and now people in the community help to look after the beaches and keep the turtles safe.

Every year, we save thousands of turtle eggs from danger. Our project really makes a difference.

Veronica

Orangutan

I volunteer at an orangutan rescue centre near my village. Orangutans are one of the most endangered animals in the world. Humans are destroying their **natural habitat** by cutting down the jungle for buildings, roads and farming.

Our centre helps orangutans which are in danger. We feed them and help the sick ones get better. It's like a school, too. We teach them how to **survive in the wild** so that when they're ready, the orangutans can go back to a safer part of the jungle.

Umar

Hummingbird

At school, I'm learning about the endangered species in my city, like the hummingbird. This little bird is in danger because the city is growing. There are more and more new buildings, so the hummingbird is losing its habitat.

I want to protect hummingbirds because I think we should help protect all endangered species. In my garden at home, we planted flowers and we hung some food and water feeders from the trees. The trees in the garden also **provide shelter** so that the birds have a safe place to build nests. I'm happy because now I see hummingbirds in our garden all the time.

Alejandro

2 **Read again and complete the table.**

	Turtles	Orangutans	Hummingbirds
Project	Turtle Protection Project	orangutan rescue centre	school project
What is the problem?	People catch turtles to sell their eggs		
How are people helping?	They look after the beaches and keep turtles safe.		

3 **Which of the projects would you like to help with? Why?**

I love hummingbirds, so I'd like to help with that project.

I'd like to help in the orangutan rescue centre because orangutans are my favourite animal.

**FIND OUT MORE**
What are the biggest causes of animal endangerment?

1 **Read the student report. How do bees help plants to survive?**

Protecting bees

Why are bees important?

Bees are so important because they help plants to survive. When a bee eats the sugary nectar from inside a flower, its hairy legs pick up some pollen. Pollen is the yellow powder on flowers. When the bee goes to another plant, it rubs some of the pollen onto it and this pollenates the plant. Without bees, some plants might disappear.

Another reason why they are important is that bees make honey. Honey is food for the bees in winter, but humans and other animals enjoy it too!

Why are bees endangered?

Bees are endangered because farmers use chemicals called pesticides on plants to kill the insects which eat them. Unfortunately, when farmers use these chemicals, they also kill bees.

How can we help?

- We should plant flowers in our gardens or on our balconies which bees like, and of course, don't use pesticides.
- We should also buy local honey. When we do this, we help beekeepers in our area.
- Lastly, let's remember to talk about bees and why they are so important.

2 **Underline the facts with when in the student report in Activity 1.**

3 **In pairs, discuss why it is important to protect endangered species and how you can help them. Complete the table in your notebook.**

Why is it important to protect endangered species?	How can we help?

Ready to write:
Go to Activity Book page 70.

Learning to write:
Facts with when
We use **when** to give facts.
When humans cut down trees, we destroy orangutans' natural habitat.
When we provide shelter, we give them a safe place to build nests.

Project

Create a fact file about an endangered animal.

8 World of sport

1 **Who wins a prize for the first time? Watch and check.**

2 **Watch again. Complete the sentences.**

1 Today's the _____ prize day.
2 Good luck in the race, _____ .
3 He's _____ over the mats.
4 He hasn't climbed over the _____ .
5 He's lost the _____ .
6 He's stopped to help a _____ .

STUDY

We**'ve done** it.
He **hasn't lost.**
Have you ever **won** a prize?
 Yes, I have. / No, I haven't.

3 **Read and choose the right words.**

1 **We're / We've** going to give the prize to the winners.
2 I've **ever / never** won any prizes!
3 **You've / You haven't** nearly finished!
4 He's **walk / walked** along the bench.
5 He **haven't / hasn't** lost.
6 We've **doing / done** it!

4 **Ask and answer.**

1 Do you think Lenny did the right thing?
2 Which is more important, winning or helping your friends?

1 Can you remember the last lesson? Watch the language video.

2 Choose words to talk about the pictures. | cook jump paint ~~start~~ walk wash |

1 They're going to start the race. | They're starting the race. | They've started the race.

 a **b**  **c**

2 **a** **b**  **c**

3 **a**  **b**  **c**

4 **a**  **b** **c**

5 **a**  **b** **c**

6 **a** **b**  **c**

3 65 **Listen and answer the questions.**

1 What has she done?
2 What have they done?
3 What has he done?
4 What has Michael done?
5 What have they done?
6 What has Robert done?

4 **Read and order the words.**

1 this / afternoon. / visited / He's / his / grandmother
2 you / Have / ever / basketball? / played
3 never / ice skating / before. / been / She's
4 He / his / hasn't / done / homework.
5 won / first / We've / prize!
6 entered / the / Have / they / competition?

Practice: present perfect   73

1 **Read the blog. What time of year do people do your favourite sport?**

ALL BLOGS   MY BLOG   NEW POST

Kid's Box
Reports

When we do some sports, we need the right weather.

Sports for all seasons

Athletics is a sport which we usually do outside. It's difficult to do in the cold and rain so, at school, we do athletics in the **summer**. Lots of people play **golf**. You play golf in any season of the year, but not when it snows!

We can only do some sports in the **winter** because we need snow and ice. A lot of people enjoy **skiing** in the winter holidays. Today a lot of young people like **snowboarding**, too. **Sledging** is also very good fun in winter. You can sledge down a hill.

There are other sports which you can do in any season. In the UK and Europe, **cycling** is a very popular sport. A lot of people cycle in **spring**, **autumn** and winter, not only in the summer. Some people have **racing** bikes and enter competitions. The most famous bicycle race is the **Tour de France**, which is in the summer.

The dates for the seasons are different in different parts of the world. In Europe, North America and Asia, spring is from March to June, but in Australia, Africa, India and South America, it is from about September to December.

2 **Read again and correct the sentences.**

1 At school they do athletics in the autumn.
2 It's easy to do athletics in the cold and rain.
3 You can play golf in the snow.
4 To do winter sports we need fog and rain.

5 People go sledging in the summer.
6 Spring comes between autumn and winter.
7 Winter comes after summer.
8 The Tour de France is a snowboarding race.

3 **Ask and answer.**

1 Which sports do you enjoy doing in the summer? Why?
2 Can you practise any of these winter sports where you live? Why?

> I enjoy playing basketball in the summer because I can play outside.

> I can go sledging where I live because it snows in the winter.

1 🎧 📝 66 **Listen and write the words.** golf

2 🎧 ▶ 67-68 **Listen and order. Listen and check. Then do karaoke.**

a Some like playing football,
Some like watching it. ☐

b We've skated in the park,
We've made a ball to throw. ☐

c We've played golf with Grandma,
We've raced against the clock. ☐

d We've skied down a mountain,
We've climbed up a rock, ☐

e We love sport, swimming, sailing, running!
We love sport,
We love to do it all. 1

f It's good to move your body,
DON'T JUST SIT! ☐

g We've played badminton and tennis,
We've sledged in the snow, ☐

3 **Read and complete. Answer the questions.**

> hill ~~mountains~~ skiing sledging
> snowball snowboard snowboarding

This morning Jane is coming home from her holiday in the ⁽¹⁾ ___mountains___
with her family. She's had a great time. During the week her mother and father
went ⁽²⁾ _____ every morning, but Jane and her older brother Frank
went ⁽³⁾ _____ . After lunch Jane and her brothers played in the snow.
They tried to play volleyball with a big ⁽⁴⁾ _____ , but it was very
difficult because the snow was too soft. On the last day they all went
⁽⁵⁾ _____ together. Jane's parents and brothers kept falling and rolling
down the ⁽⁶⁾ _____ , but Jane was quite good at it. She wants to buy a
⁽⁷⁾ _____ and go to the mountains again next year.

1 Where did Jane go on holiday?
2 Who did she go with?
3 What did her parents do every morning?
4 Which of Jane's brothers went sledging with her?
5 What did they try to play volleyball with?
6 What did they all do on the last day of their holiday?

Sounds and life skills
Working together

 1 ▶ **Watch the video. How does Lenny feel? How does Lenny's friend feel?**

Pronunciation focus

 2 🎧 **69 Listen and write the words in the correct form.**

STELLA: Yeah! He's _____ (jump) over the mats
and he's _____ (walk) along the bench,
but he hasn't _____ (climb) over the wall.
Come on, Lenny! You've nearly _____
(finish)!

 3 🎧 **70 Listen to the verbs. Complete the table.**

/t/ ending	/d/ ending	
		decided
		wanted
		needed
		waited

 4 Lenny is talking to his friend in the race. Read and match.

1 Hey, are you alright?
2 Would you like some help?
3 OK. If you hold the rope, I can push you up.
4 There you go!

a Good idea!
b Yes, I think so.
c Thank you so much!
d Yes, please!

 5 In a group, complete the teamwork challenge.

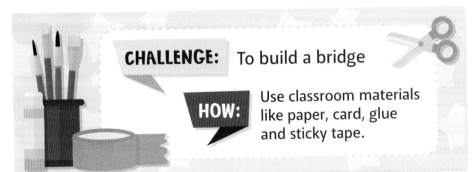

CHALLENGE: To build a bridge

HOW: Use classroom materials like paper, card, glue and sticky tape.

Useful language
Would you like …?
If you …, I can …
Let's …

Diggory Bones

Now what have you done?

You should close your mouth, Brutus! Those butterflies are dangerous!

The butterflies have started to go back to the walls.

This looks like the way out. It's the first time anyone's used this door.

Wait for me!

TLING TLING

I don't know what's inside, so stay right behind me. Don't try to bring anything with you!

I haven't touched anything.

Hmm. They've painted sports on these walls ... they're trying to tell us something.

The Ancient Egyptians loved sport.

The Ancient Egyptians invented hockey and handball. You should use some of those treasures.

You need more exercise, Brutus.

I've waited for this moment all my life ... I'm going to be rich!

When the water comes, swim up to the light.

Right.

BOOOM

GLOO GLOO

Time to go, Dad!

GURGLE

No! my gold!

The Ancient Story of Sirius says you can't take the treasure and live, Brutus.

I got your email, son. The first one you've ever sent from a snake bowl, eh?

Thanks, Dad!

Brutus hasn't come up!

POLICE

my treasure! I've lost it all!

You're the 'treasure' now, Brutus!

⭐ 1 **Which sports did the Ancient Egyptians invent? Where did Diggory send the email from?**

Story: unit language in context 77

How do people train for different sports?

1 🎧 72 **Listen and read. Which sport should you do with a trainer?**

LET'S GET ACTIVE!

Sports and exercise are very healthy hobbies, which people enjoy all over the world. There are so many different types to choose from, but did you know that there are two types of exercise? There's **aerobic** exercise, which means 'with air' and **anaerobic** exercise, which means 'without air'. Let's find out more.

LONG-DISTANCE RUNNING

This is a great example of aerobic sport. When you run you need to **breathe** faster and deeper, so **oxygen** travels from your **lungs** to your **heart**. Then your heart sends oxygen around your body to your **muscles**, and this gives them energy. If you want to be a long-distance runner, it's important to train slowly. Every time you train, your heart and lungs get stronger, and this makes you fitter, so you can run further and for longer. Try it, and who knows? One day you might run a marathon!

WEIGHTLIFTING

This is an anaerobic sport where weightlifters do short, repeated and very difficult exercises for about 90 seconds. There's no time for oxygen to get to their muscles before the exercise is finished, so their body has to use the energy it already has. This means they must take lots of breaks. Weightlifters use all the **muscle groups**, which is why their bodies are so strong. If you want to try weightlifting, it's important to ask a sports teacher for help. If you do an exercise incorrectly, it's easy to get hurt.

HOCKEY

Lastly, like most sports, hockey is both aerobic and anaerobic. When a player runs across the field, they use aerobic energy, and when they hit the ball, they use anaerobic energy.

Think about other sports and the types of energy they use. Try a new sport today and comment below! Happy exercising!

2 **Read again and choose the correct word.**

1 It makes you fitter.   (aerobic) / anaerobic

2 It uses oxygen.   aerobic / anaerobic

3 It uses energy from the body.   aerobic / anaerobic

4 It is a long exercise.   aerobic / anaerobic

5 It is short exercises.   aerobic / anaerobic

6 It makes your muscles stronger.   aerobic / anaerobic

3 **What sports do you like doing and why?**

> I like playing cricket because it makes me fit and I can play with my friends at the same time.

> I exercise every day, and I really like gymnastics because it makes me stronger.

FIND OUT MORE
What is the most popular sport in your country? Is it mostly aerobic or anaerobic?

Physical education: aerobic and anaerobic exercise | 🛡 critical thinking

1 **Read the leaflet. Why is swimming a good hobby?**

DID YOU KNOW...?

The fastest time recorded for an athlete to complete a marathon while running backwards is 3:43:39.

Try swimming

It's never too late to try swimming, and there are lots of reasons why it's an amazing sport. Firstly, water is all around us, so it's important to know how to be safe in and near water.

Another reason why you should go swimming is that it is very, very healthy. Swimming is an intense aerobic workout. It uses lots of different muscle groups, so it's a great way to get fitter and stronger.

Finally, swimming is a great sport to do both alone and in a team. You can swim alone and take some time to think about your day, and you can make some new friends and enter competitions as a team. It's so much fun!

If you're a beginner, or maybe you haven't been swimming for a long time, get back in that pool and enjoy it. It's such a healthy hobby!

2 **Underline words that help organise the writer's ideas in the leaflet in Activity 1.**

Learning to write:

Organising ideas

We use **firstly**, **first of all**, **secondly**, **another reason is**, **lastly** and **finally** to organise ideas.

First of all, football is a great team sport.

Lastly, like most sports, hockey is both aerobic and anaerobic.

3 **In pairs, discuss other sports and why they are good. Write your ideas in your notebook.**

Ready to write:

Go to Activity Book page 78.

Project

Research a sport and make a poster to present to the class.

1 **Look at the picture. Talk about it in pairs.**

> It's a sunny day.

> The little boy is playing with a red car.

Daisy

Sally

Vicky

Fred

John

Paul

Jack

2 🎧 73 **Listen and draw lines. There is one example.**

3 **Read the story. Choose the right words and write them on the lines.**

> are   can   clothes   dangerous   Have   ~~kicked~~
> quiet   sandwiches   shouldn't   water

I went to the beach with Sam and his dad last weekend.
We took a picnic and a ball. We were playing football on the
beach when I ____kicked____ the ball into the sea! It was
soon far out in the (1) _____ !
'Can you swim?' Sam asked.
'No, I've never learnt to swim!' I answered. 'Can you swim?'
'Yes,' said Sam, and he started swimming.
The waves were huge.
Sam's dad started shouting at him, (2) '_____ you
seen the flag? You shouldn't swim when there is a red flag!' Sam's dad swam towards him and pulled
him back to the beach.
'Sorry, Dad,' Sam said. 'The sea was (3) _____ !'
'Er. Shall we have our picnic, now?' I said.
We went to get our picnic, but it wasn't there.
'You (4) _____ leave food on the beach!' Sam's dad said. 'The birds always eat it. Look!'
It was true. We saw lots of big white birds eating our (5) _____ .

Now choose the best name for the story. Tick (✓) one box.

A day at the beach ☐

The dangerous birds ☐

A lovely swim ☐

4 Play the game.

What's the question?

Instructions: Play in pairs. One player is **red** and the other is **blue**. In turns, go round the board. Read the answer and ask the question. **If your question is right**, score 3 points, **if it's wrong**, lose 1 point. Make a note of the points in your notebook.

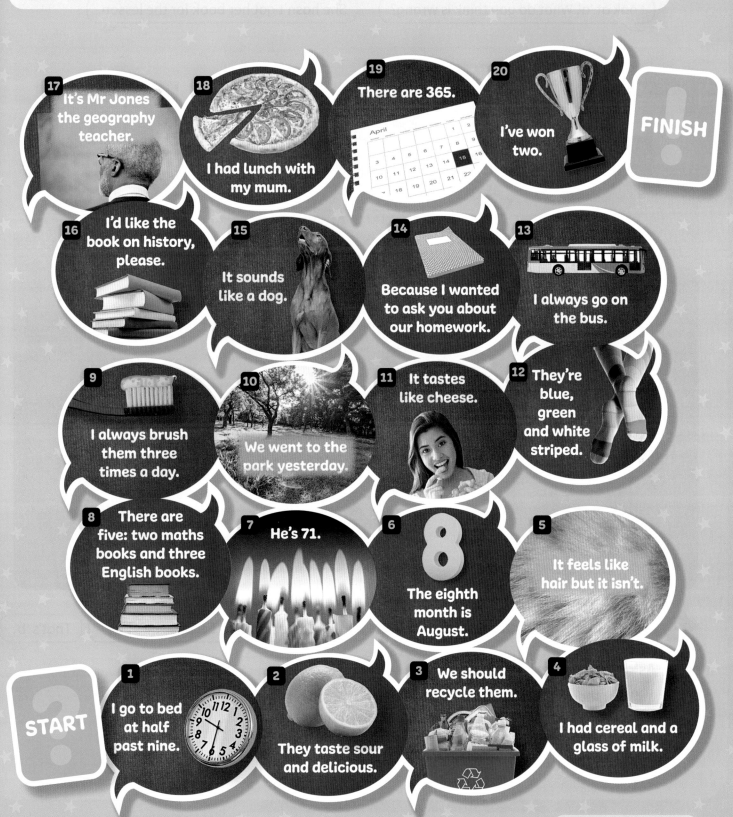

17 It's Mr Jones the geography teacher.

18 I had lunch with my mum.

19 There are 365.

20 I've won two.

FINISH

16 I'd like the book on history, please.

15 It sounds like a dog.

14 Because I wanted to ask you about our homework.

13 I always go on the bus.

9 I always brush them three times a day.

10 We went to the park yesterday.

11 It tastes like cheese.

12 They're blue, green and white striped.

8 There are five: two maths books and three English books.

7 He's 71.

6 8 The eighth month is August.

5 It feels like hair but it isn't.

START

1 I go to bed at half past nine.

2 They taste sour and delicious.

3 We should recycle them.

4 I had cereal and a glass of milk.

1 **Look at the picture. What's wrong? Talk to your friends.**

> Look at 'a'. What do you think is wrong?

> She hasn't got her book for the lesson.

2 🎧 74 **Listen and check. Say the letter.** > 🎧 1 He's worried because he's late. > That's 'b'.

3 **Ask and answer.**

1 What should the children do to start their lesson on time?
2 Which of the things in the picture do you never do?
3 Which of the things in the picture do you sometimes do?
4 What should you do to be a better student?

Values: Units 1 & 2 Respect in the classroom | 🛡 social responsibilities

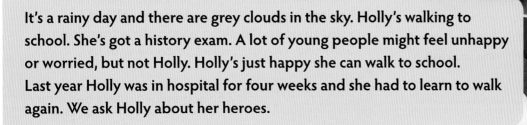

1 Read and answer the questions.

1 How did Holly break her leg?
2 Why did she hit her head?
3 Who helped her?

Holly's heroes

It's a rainy day and there are grey clouds in the sky. Holly's walking to school. She's got a history exam. A lot of young people might feel unhappy or worried, but not Holly. Holly's just happy she can walk to school. Last year Holly was in hospital for four weeks and she had to learn to walk again. We ask Holly about her heroes.

So, Holly, can you tell us what happened to you last year?

I was cycling home from my friend's house after school. It was dark and I didn't have any lights so I couldn't see clearly. I was going very quickly down a hill near my block of flats, when suddenly a cat ran across the road in front of me. I tried not to hit it, but I fell off my bike.

How terrible! Then what happened?

Well, I can't remember. I hit my head because I wasn't wearing a helmet. People told me what happened. I fell badly and broke my leg in two places.

How did you get to hospital?

A driver saw me on the ground and stopped his car. He phoned for an ambulance, and they took me to the nearest hospital. I arrived in less than ten minutes.

Wow! That was fast.

Yes. Thanks to them, the doctors and nurses could work quickly. I had an X-ray and then they had to operate for four hours, but they saved my leg. Then I had to learn to walk again.

So you've got a lot of heroes: the ambulance drivers, and the team of doctors and nurses.

Yes, but also the driver who stopped to call the ambulance. I want to say thank you to everyone who helped me. When I grow up, I want to be a doctor or nurse because I'd like to help other people too.

2 🎧 **75** Listen and say 'fire fighter', 'doctor', 'police officer' or 'ambulance driver'.

Units 5&6 Values Tell the truth but don't hurt

1 **Read and choose answers.**

1
Your friend's got a new haircut and you think it looks awful. When he asks you what you think, you say:

a 'It looks terrible. I don't like it.'
b 'It's OK but I prefer the old haircut.'
c 'It looks amazing! It's perfect for you.'

2
Your mum spent all afternoon making a special dinner, but you don't like it. What do you do?

a You eat it and ask for more.
b You make a horrible face and say you don't want to eat it.
c You tell her that it's nice, but it's not your favourite meal. Suggest a meal that she can make more quickly and easily.

3
You're shopping with a friend who wants to buy a new dress. She tries on a dress that looks awful on her. She asks you what you think. What do you do?

a You say the dress doesn't look very nice and you find a different dress for her to try.
b You say that the dress looks lovely and tell her to buy it.
c You tell her the dress looks horrible and you're bored with shopping.

4
A new boy in your class invites you to play tennis on Saturday afternoon. You'd like to go to the cinema with some friends. What do you do?

a You say, 'Sorry, I can't. I want to go to the cinema with my friends.'
b You make a horrible face and say, 'I hate tennis!'
c You smile and say, 'Thanks very much but I want to go to the cinema with some friends on Saturday. Would you like to come with us?'

5
You've got a friend who sometimes smells bad after the sports lesson. What's the best way to help him?

a Make a horrible face and say, 'You smell bad. Have a shower!'
b Give him a box of shower gel and deodorant for his birthday.
c Talk about him with the other students and laugh.

6
Your dad hasn't got a job. He lost it last year and your parents are worried about money. It's your birthday soon and you want a big party, but your parents say that you can't have one this year. What do you do?

a You tell your parents that you understand and it isn't important.
b You get angry and stay in your room all day.
c You tell your parents that you understand. You ask your friends to bring some lemonade and crisps to the park, so you can have a small party.

2 **Talk about your answers with your partner. Are they the same or different?**

3 **Discuss these questions.**

1 Why is it important to tell the truth?
2 What is trust and why is it important?
3 How can we tell our friends and family the truth and not hurt their feelings?

1 Read the letters and answer the questions.

Dear Betty and Robert,

I work really hard at school and I always study a lot for my exams, but I don't get good marks. I don't fail, but I get 5, 6 or sometimes 7 out of 10.

My best friend, Emma, gets the best marks in the school, but she cheats. She takes photos of the book on her mobile phone and uses them in the exams. I'm really unhappy about this.

Should I do the same as my friend and get better marks or should I tell the teacher that she cheats in exams? Please help me to decide.

Yours,

Nico

Dear Nico,

When you work hard at school and study for your exams, you are learning things. I'm sorry that you don't get the good marks that you want. It's better to work hard and learn things than cheat and learn very little. It's not a good idea for you to do the same as Emma. You should feel good because you're passing your exams. Do your best and don't worry about other people's marks.

This situation is difficult. You don't have to tell the teacher that your friend is cheating. Emma can't always cheat — one day someone is going to catch her.

Yours,

Betty and Robert

1 Does Nico work hard at school?
2 Does he get good marks?
3 How does Emma cheat in the exams?
4 What do Betty and Robert think about cheating?
5 Do they think that Nico should get the same marks as other students?

2 Read the letter. Discuss these questions.

1 Is Sarah right to be unhappy? Why?
2 What do you think Katya should do?
3 What do you think Sarah should do?

Dear Betty and Robert,

I'm really unhappy because I've made a huge mistake with my best friend Sarah. There's a group of very popular girls in my class. They're cool and funny and everyone wants to be friends with them. They asked me to go out with them last Saturday. I was really excited, but it was Sarah's birthday.

I didn't go to Sarah's party and now she's unhappy with me. Now she doesn't want to be my friend. I've started to see that the popular girls are boring and unkind, and I don't like going out with them. I want to be Sarah's best friend again. What should I do?

Yours,

Katya

Grammar reference

1

What's the time?

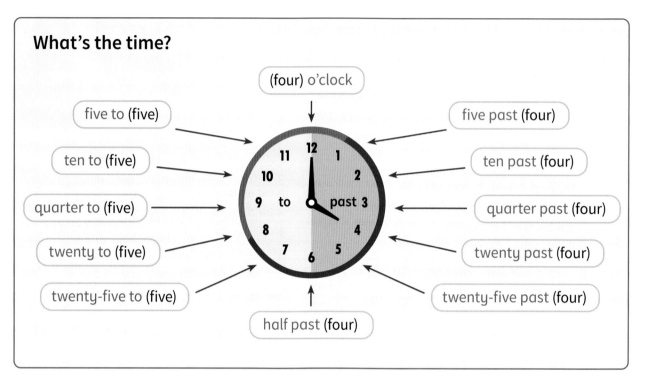

(four) o'clock

five to (five)
ten to (five)
quarter to (five)
twenty to (five)
twenty-five to (five)

five past (four)
ten past (four)
quarter past (four)
twenty past (four)
twenty-five past (four)

half past (four)

2

We use *going to* to talk and write about the future.

Affirmative	Negative (n't = not)	Question
I'm going to work **hard**.	I'm not going to work **hard**.	Am I going to work **hard**?
She's going to work **hard**.	She isn't going to work **hard**.	Is she going to work **hard**?
They're going to work **hard**.	They aren't going to work **hard**.	Are they going to work **hard**?

3

right	⌐→	She turned right.
left	←⌐	They took the second street on the left.
across	⬆	They looked and listened carefully before they walked across the street.
along	→	We walked along the street.
straight on	⬆	He didn't turn. He drove straight on to the end of the road.
corner	←⌐	I turned at the corner.
past	□↑	You have to walk past the park.

We use the past continuous to describe what was happening in the past.

Affirmative	Negative (n't = not)	Question
I was reading a book.	I wasn't reading a book.	Was I reading a book?
We were reading a book.	We weren't reading a book.	Were we reading a book?

We use *made of* to describe materials.

Affirmative	Negative (n't = not)	Question
It's made of metal.	It isn't made of metal.	Is it made of metal?
They're made of metal.	They aren't made of metal.	Are they made of metal?

We use verb + *like* to describe things.

Affirmative	Negative (n't = not)	Question
It sounds like a train.	It doesn't sound like a train.	Does it sound like a train?
They sound like cats.	They don't sound like cats.	Do they sound like cats?

We use *should* to give and ask for help or advice.

Affirmative	Negative (n't = not)	Question
I should tell my teacher.	I shouldn't tell my teacher.	Should I tell my teacher?
He should tell his teacher.	He shouldn't tell his teacher.	Should he tell his teacher?

We use the present perfect to talk and write about things we did any time up to now.

Affirmative	Negative (n't = not)	Question
She's visited London.	She hasn't visited London.	Has she visited London?
They've visited London.	They haven't visited London.	Have they visited London?

Flyers Listening Part 1

1 🎧 76 **Describe the two pictures. Listen and circle A or B.**

Picture A   Picture B

1 A **B**

2 A B

3 A B

4 A B

5 A B

6 A B

2 🎧 77 🐵 **Listen and draw lines. There is one example.**

Betty   William   George   Sophia

Holly   Richard   Oliver

Flyers Listening Part 4

1 🎧 78 **Listen and draw arrows → ↑ ↗ .**

START

FINISH

2 🎧 79 🐵 **Listen and tick (✓) the box. There is one example.**

When did Uncle David last see George?

A ☐   B ☐   C ✓

1 What's George's favourite subject?

A ☐   B ☐   C ☐

2 Which project is George doing at school now?

A ☐   B ☐   C ☐

3 Where did George go on his last school trip?

A ☐   B ☐   C ☐

4 Which instrument is George's sister learning to play?

A ☐   B ☐   C ☐

5 What job does George want to do in the future?

A ☐   B ☐   C ☐

Flyers Listening Part 5

1 🎧 80 **Talk about the differences. Listen and circle. Then complete the sentences.**

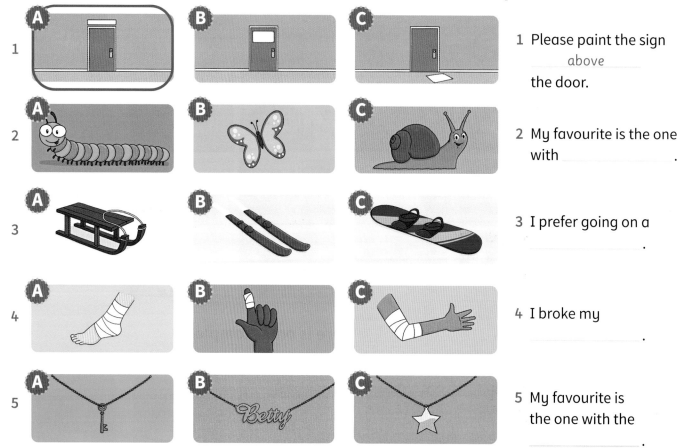

1 Please paint the sign ___above___ the door.

2 My favourite is the one with _____.

3 I prefer going on a _____.

4 I broke my _____.

5 My favourite is the one with the _____.

2 🎧 81 🐵 **Listen and colour and write. There is one example.**

HISTORY MUSEUM

Flyers Reading and Writing Part 1

1 Look. Use the code to colour the squares.

passenger	ambulance	wood	trainers	astronaut	wool
passenger	uniform	pilot	skiing	fridge	pyjamas
rocket	bandage	golf	platform	airport	cooker
station	oven	planet	medicine	glass	swimming

Key:
clothes = brown
space = yellow
air travel = blue
train travel = purple
sport = green
hospital = pink
kitchen = orange
materials = grey

2 Look and read. Choose the correct words and write them on the lines. There is one example.

a railway

pyjamas

trainers

a platform

a mechanic

envelopes

metal

a bridge

	This person flies a plane and usually wears a uniform.	a pilot	~~a pilot~~
1	People travel in cars along these large roads when they go on long journeys.		
2	This is the name for a person who travels on a plane or train, or in a taxi.		pockets
3	People walk over this when they want to cross a road or river.		
4	You can stay in this when you are camping in the countryside.		stamps
5	People usually wear these on their feet when they go running or play a sport.		a passenger
6	You can find these on coats and jackets. People put things like keys and money into them.		a tent
7	This material comes from sheep and people often use it to make sweaters.		
8	This person repairs cars and other machines.		motorways
9	You walk along this in a station when you get on or off a train.		
10	You put letters inside these and write the addresses on the front.		wool

Flyers Reading and Writing Part 3

1 Read and guess the missing word. Is it a verb, singular noun, plural noun, adverb or adjective?

1 My dad's not going to ___play (verb)___ golf today because it's windy. He says a ___storm (noun)___ is coming.

2 I didn't like sleeping in a _____. You can hear a lot of _____ animals at night.

3 There weren't many _____ on the train so we sat next to the _____ and enjoyed the views.

4 We watched an _____ documentary last night about butterflies that _____ thousands of kilometres every winter.

5 My cousins _____ walking across the bridge when they saw dolphins in the _____.

6 Yesterday, my sister and I made a _____ cake but we forgot to add sugar! It wasn't very _____!

2 Read the story. Choose a word from the box. Write the correct word next to numbers 1–5. There is one example.

~~competition~~   friendly   already   new   invitation   filmed   time   exciting   date   wrote

Last night, when Oliver and Sophia were leaving the cinema, they saw a poster about a music ___competition___. The manager of a famous TV music show was looking for a young rock band to be in a (1) _____ film. They had to send a video to the email address on the poster.

Oliver and Sophia were in a band. Oliver played the piano, Sophia was the singer and the two other members, Harry and Emma, played the guitar.

Oliver showed them the poster on his phone at school the next day. "But look at the (2) _____!" said Harry. "We need to send the video before 17th April. That's tomorrow!"

"Let's make a video of our new song, 'Foggy Days', right now," said Emma.

Sophia's brother borrowed his dad's camera. He (3) _____ the band on the school stage and emailed the video after school. A month later, they found out that their song didn't win. They were all unhappy, but Emma said, "It doesn't matter, our band is (4) _____ famous at school!"

The next day, a different TV manager phoned Emma. "I'd like to play your song at the beginning of our weather news," he said, "When it's foggy, of course!"

"Wow!" laughed Oliver. "That's (5) _____ news!" Everyone agreed.

(6) **Now choose the best name for the story. Tick (✓) one box.**

☐ A special music video.   ☐ A song on TV.

☐ Rock band winners!

Flyers Reading and Writing Part 5

1 Read and complete so the two sentences have the same meaning. You can use 1, 2, 3 or 4 words.

1 Sarah really didn't like storms because she was scared of lightning.

_____Lightening_____ frightened Sarah.

2 One night, when Yuna was camping with her family, there was a strange sound and she got up.

Yuna got up when she heard a _____.

3 Kito and his family were happy when they put their shopping in the car and drove home.

The family went home happily after they had _____ in the car.

2 🐵 **Look at the picture and read the story. Write some words to complete the sentences about the story. You can use 1, 2, 3 or 4 words.**

The students in Class 6A were excited as they woke up on the first morning of their school skiing trip. They all got dressed and hurried to have breakfast as fast as they could. The mountains around the hotel looked amazing.

"What time do the skiing classes start?" asked Robert. "It's going to be so much fun!"

Their teacher, Mrs West, looked worried but smiled and said, "I have some bad news and some good news."

The bad news was that there was no skiing for the first three days because the snow was too deep. But the good news was that a pair of eagles was making their nest between some rocks on the highest mountain. Many people thought this kind of eagle was extinct.

"There mustn't be any activity on the mountains at this time," Mrs West explained, "but we can do a project about eagles instead."

"We studied extinct animals in our science lessons, and it was really interesting," said Robert.

The students were also happy when they found out that there was ice on a lake behind the hotel so everyone could have ice skating classes for three days.

"It was funny when we actually started our skiing classes," Helen told her mum when she was back home. "We kept falling over all the time because we were watching the eagles flying above us!"

Examples

It was the first day of the students' _____skiing trip_____.

The students wanted to eat _____breakfast_____ quickly.

Questions

1 The students could see _____ outside the hotel.

2 The teacher told them they couldn't go _____ for several days.

3 She also told them some _____ about eagles.

4 The nests weren't easy to see because they were high up _____.

5 The students already knew about _____ from their science classes.

6 The students were pleased they could go _____ on the lake.

7 Many students looked up at the eagles during their skiing classes and _____ a lot.

Flyers Speaking Part 1

1 **Listen and circle the differences in picture 2. Then listen and respond. Complete the sentences about picture 1.**

Picture 1

Picture 2

In picture 1, …

1 two children are   _making a fire_ .
2 a man in the stream is _____ of two butterflies.
3 a girl is _____ the bridge.
4 the boy's _____ are in a rucksack.
5 there are _____ with a path.
6 a boy is _____ under a tree.

2 🎧 83 🐵 **Listen. Talk about the differences. Listen again to check your answers.**

Flyers Speaking Part 2

1 Look at the picture. Ask and answer with a partner.

Where / castle?   Where / mum and daughter go?   Who / walk dog?   What time?

How many children / get on bus?   What old woman / pull?   What girl / read?

Sunny or foggy?

2 🎧 84 🐵 Listen. Answer the questions about William's journey. Then ask questions about Katy's journey.

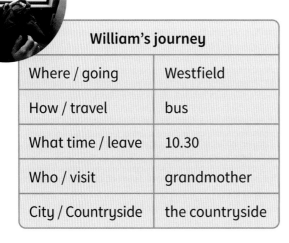

William's journey	
Where / going	Westfield
How / travel	bus
What time / leave	10.30
Who / visit	grandmother
City / Countryside	the countryside

Katy's journey	
Where / going	?
How / travel	?
What time / leave	?
Who / visit	?
City / Countryside	?

Thanks and Acknowledgements

Authors' thanks

Many thanks to everyone at Cambridge University Press and Assessment for their dedication and hard work, and in particular to:

Louise Wood for doing such a great job overseeing the level; Catriona Brownlee for her dedication and sound editorial judgement; freelance editors Melissa Bryant and Sarah Jane Lewis.

We would also like to thank all our pupils and colleagues, past, present and future, at Star English academy in Murcia, especially Jim Kelly for his friendship and support throughout the years.

Dedications

For Jim Kelly: Here's to the next thirty years of our Starship enterprise. – CN

To my Murcian family: Adolfo and Isabel, the Peinado sisters and their other halves for always treating me so well, thanks for being there and for making my life in Murcia so much fun. – MT

Illustration

Antonio Cuesta; Dave Williams, Ana Sebastian (Bright Agency); David Belmont, Javier Joaquin, Laszlo Veres, Moreno Chiacchiera (Beehive); Shahab (Sylvie Poggio Artists).

Audio

Audio production by Sounds Like Mike Ltd.

Video

Video acknowledgements are in the Teacher Resources on Cambridge One.

Design and typeset

Blooberry Design

Additional authors

Rebecca Legros and Robin Thompson (CLIL); Montse Watkin (Sounds and life skills, Exam folder)

The authors and publishers acknowledge the following sources of copyright material and are grateful for the permissions granted. While every effort has been made, it has not always been possible to identify the sources of all the material used, or to trace all copyright holders. If any omissions are brought to our notice, we will be happy to include the appropriate acknowledgments on reprinting and in the next update to the digital edition, as applicable.

Key: U = Unit, R = Review, V = Values

Photography

All the photos are sourced from Getty Images.

U0: Compassionate Eye Foundation/Martin Barraud/Stone; teekid/E+; mediaphotos/iStock/Getty Images Plus; Ableimages/DigitalVision; FatCamera/E+; Monty Rakusen/Image Source; ullstein bild; PhotoMelon/iStock/Getty Images Plus; Martin Barraud/Stone; iLexx/iStock/Getty Images Plus; AndreaAstes/iStock/Getty Images Plus; Brennan Bucannan/EyeEm; Print Collector/Hulton Archive; allanswart/iStock/Getty Images; Roman Bykhalets/iStock/Getty Images Plus; SMSka/iStock/Getty Images Plus; MsMoloko/iStock/Getty Images Plus; **U1:** ZargonDesign/E+; metamorworks/iStock/Getty Images Plus; all images copyright of Jamie Lamb - elusive-images.co.uk/Moment; Dmytro Aksonov/E+; CBS Photo Archive; simonkr/E+; Tony Garcia/Image Source; Marc Dufresne/E+; pigphoto/iStock/Getty Images Plus; angie marie photography/Moment; EXTREME-PHOTOGRAPHER/iStock/Getty Images Plus; Richard Newstead/Moment; Mark Stevenson/Stocktrek Images; Reinhard Dirscherl/The Image Bank; Dgwildlife/iStock/Getty Images Plus; FARBAI/iStock/Getty Images Plus; **U2:** monkeybusinessimages/iStock/Getty Images Plus; FatCamera/iStock/Getty Images Plus; Mahmud013/E+; Guy Cali/Corbis; Maskot; Erik Isakson/Tetra images; miodrag ignjatovic/E+; AleksandarNakic/E+; David Madison/Stone; adoc-photos/Corbis Historical; Aitor Alcalde Colomer/Getty Images Sport; Larry Marano/Getty Images Entertainment; Kent Nishimura/Los Angeles Times; Bloomberg; filmstudio/E+; sinology/Moment; Lacheev/iStock/Getty Images Plus; Yellow Dog Productions/The Image Bank; Westend61; Somyot Techapuwapat/Moment; Jose A. Bernat Bacete/Moment; PATRICK T. FALLON/AFP; CZQS2000/STS/Photodisc; Peter Dazeley/The Image Bank; Chonticha Vatpongpee/EyeEm; Jose A. Bernat Bacete/Moment; syntika/iStock/Getty Images Plus; eyewave/iStock/Getty Images Plus; **U3:** SOPA Images/LightRocket; _ultraforma_/iStock Unreleased; Andrea Pistolesi/Stone; Sara Amroussi/EyeEm; Sergio Amiti/Moment; aapsky/iStock/Getty Images Plus; Vladislav Zolotov/iStock/Getty Images Plus; BaMa/Photographer's Choice RF; Cris CantÃ³n/Moment; DANNY HU/Moment; Â© Allard Schager/Moment; Blake Callahan/Moment; Hiroshi Higuchi/The Image Bank Unreleased; Caroline Purser/The Image Bank; SERGII IAREMENKO/SCIENCE PHOTO LIBRARY/Science Photo Library; aleksei-veprev/iStock/Getty Images Plus; LisLud/iStock/Getty Images Plus; **U4:** Aaron Foster/The Image Bank; omgimages/iStock/Getty Images Plus; Jamie Grill/The Image Bank; Design Pics/Ron Nickel; Tempura/E+; Ascent Xmedia/Stone; Imgorthand/E+; Neustockimages/E+; Jeff Greenough/Tetra images; John Parrot/Stocktrek Images; Historical/Corbis Historical; Juanmonino/E+; Westend61; Haje Jan Kamps/EyeEm; shannonstent/E+; Matt Anderson Photography/Moment; MARK GARLICK/SCIENCE PHOTO LIBRARY; RomanKhomlyak/iStock/Getty Images Plus; James L. Amos/Corbis Documentary; Roc Canals/Moment; Anna Sviridenko/iStock/Getty Images Plus; Lucie Kasparova/iStock/Getty Images Plus; **U5:** StratosGiannikos/iStock/Getty Images Plus; iakovenko/iStock/Getty Images Plus; artefy/iStock/Getty Images Plus; Smith Chetanachan/EyeEm; malerapaso/iStock/Getty Images Plus; Jena Ardell/Moment; Aleksandr Zubkov/Moment; DonNichols/E+; benedek/E+; Rajanish Kakade/AP; Daniel_M/iStock/Getty Images Plus; AFP; Marina Inoue/Moment; Jamroen Jaiman/EyeEm; J_rg Lcking/EyeEm; ThomasVogel/E+; Nattapol Sritongcom/EyeEm; IlexImage/E+; Jurgita Vaicikeviciene/EyeEm; Mohamad Faizal Ramli/EyeEm; malerapaso/E+; Wong Sze Fei/EyeEm; WYSIWYG/500px; fotoember/iStock Editorial; Michael Roberts/Moment Unreleased; Education Images/Universal Images Group; Paul Biris/Moment Open; Justin Case/The Image Bank; noppadon_sangpeam/iStock/Getty Images Plus; ExpressIPhoto/iStock/Getty Images Plus; Fajar Pramudianto/iStock/Getty Images Plus; **U6:** Nikola Vukicevic/iStock/Getty Images Plus; Xvision/Moment; Elena Levchenko/EyeEm; Paolo Cordoni/EyeEm; Richard Sharrocks/Moment; Andrea La Civita/EyeEm; Westend61; Nitat Termmee/Moment; piranka/E+; Dorling Kindersley/Dorling Kindersley RF; Tom-Kichi/iStock/Getty Images Plus; Peter Cade/Stone; George Karbus Photography/Image Source; John Short/Design Pics; Images By Tang Ming Tung/DigitalVision; REDA\u0026CO/Universal Images Group; SENRYU/iStock/Getty Images Plus; **U7:** George Pachantouris/Moment; Seamind Panadda/EyeEm; Picture by Tambako the Jaguar/Moment; EcoPic/iStock/Getty Images Plus; Ed Reschke/Stone; Jasius/Moment; Ceneri/DigitalVision Vectors; Tim Grist Photography/Moment; Jordan Lye/Moment; FotoDuets/iStock/Getty Images Plus; Dimijana/iStock/Getty Images Plus; Voyagerix/iStock/Getty Images Plus; bradleym/E+; elenabs/iStock/Getty Images Plus; AlexeyBlogoodf/iStock/Getty Images Plus; Ekaterina Bedoeva/iStock/Getty Images Plus; Dawid Lech/foap; Nataliia Korzina/EyeEm; USO/iStock/Getty Images Plus; Linda Krueger/500Px Plus; schnuddel/E+; porojnicu/iStock/Getty Images Plus; Trudie Davidson/Moment; **U8:** DieterMeyrl/E+; Janie Airey/Image Source; sonyae/iStock/Getty Images Plus; mbbirdy/E+; pyotr021/iStock/Getty Images Plus; Imgorthand/E+; Cavan Images; Blend Images - Erik Isakson/Tetra images; SDI Productions/E+; triloks/E+; sot/Photodisc; Â© Marco Bottigelli/Moment; Westend61/Brand X Pictures; FatCamera/E+; quavondo/E+; cjp/E+; luplupme/iStock/Getty Images Plus; Kai-Otto Melau/Getty Images Sport; Hirurg/E+; Augustas Cetkauskas/EyeEm; Jason Hosking/Corbis; **R12:** izusek/iStock/Getty Images Plus; **R34:** David Goddard/Getty Images News; P A Thompson/The Image Bank; Jose Luis Pelaez Inc/DigitalVision; **R56:** Nikada/E+; Zoonar RF; DNY59/E+; Peerayot/iStock/Getty Images Plus; Vasko/E+; AlexandrMoroz/iStock/Getty Images Plus; Nattawut Lakjit/EyeEm; lunglee/iStock/Getty Images Plus; yorkfoto/iStock/Getty Images Plus; Gorlov/iStock/Getty Images Plus; R.Tsubin/Moment; Sjo/E+; Mika Mika/Moment; Alex Savochkin/500px; Suradech14/iStock/Getty Images Plus; Peter Dazeley/The Image Bank; Yevgen Romanenko/Moment; dashu83/iStock/Getty Images Plus; Jamroen Jaiman/EyeEm; Adha Ghazali/EyeEm; Athitat Shinagowin/EyeEm; evemilla/E+; LauriPatterson/iStock/Getty Images Plus; bortonia/E+; Issarawat Tattong/Moment; gdagys/E+; -MG-/E+; zhongyanjiang/iStock/Getty Images Plus; Ociacia/iStock/Getty Images Plus; TanyaRozhnovskaya/iStock/Getty Images Plus; Eskay Lim/EyeEm; koto_feja/iStock/Getty Images Plus; Riddy/iStock/Getty Images Plus; JohnGollop/iStock/Getty Images Plus; rudchenko/iStock/Getty Images Plus; Jamesmcq24/E+; Sittichai Karimpard/EyeEm; **R78:** Glowimages; Brockswood/iStock/Getty Images Plus; benimage/E+; subjug/iStock/Getty Images Plus; Cavan Images/iStock/Getty Images Plus; Cimmerian/E+; pagadesign/E+; Tetra Images/Tetra images; Kyrylo Glivin/EyeEm; Caspar Benson/fStop; shunli zhao/Moment; Jose Luis Pelaez Inc/DigitalVision; artpipi/E+; sound35/iStock/Getty Images Plus; Talaj/iStock/Getty Images Plus; vauvau/iStock/Getty Images Plus; Gannet77/E+; Hill Street Studios/DigitalVision; Iurii Korolev/iStock/Getty Images Plus; onurdongel/iStock/Getty Images Plus; luoman/E+; powerofforever/iStock/Getty Images Plus; **V34:** Gary John Norman/DigitalVision; **V78:** Sam Edwards/OJO Images; FARBAI/iStock/Getty Images Plus; **EF:** FamVeld/iStock/Getty Images Plus; Nahhan/iStock/Getty Images Plus; Empato/E+; Prasit photo/Moment; jsmith/iStock/Getty Images Plus; CreativeNature_nl/iStock/Getty Images Plus; Andrew Holt/The Image Bank; Jovo Marjanovic/EyeEm; MR1805/iStock/Getty Images Plus; Digital Zoo/DigitalVision; Peter Rahm/EyeEm; Serkan Erol/EyeEm; Sergio Amiti/Moment; Turnervisual/E+; d3sign/Moment; Mike Kemp/Tetra images; Â© Marco Bottigelli/Moment; Imgorthand/E+; Hanna Shyriaieva/iStock/Getty Images Plus; Kyle Lee/EyeEm.

The following photographs are sourced from other sources/libraries.

U1: Pictorial Press Ltd/Alamy Stock Photo; **U2:** Luciano Cosmo/Shutterstock; **U4:** Andrea Danti/Shutterstock; **U7:** Matthijs Kuijpers/Alamy Stock Photo; **U8:** Ian Middleton/Alamy Stock Photo.

Cover photography by Tiffany Mumford for Creative Listening.

Commissioned photography by Stephen Noble and Duncan Yeldham for Creative Listening.